Johnny Cooper – Championship Manager

The Story of Mansfield Town FC 99/00*

*(according to Championship Manager)

This book is dedicated to Simon Saliger, who introduced me to *Champ Man* in 1992, Nick Braxton-Abery who was my first and most dedicated *Champ Man* co-player and Ollie Denbigh, who nearly ruined his A-Levels due to this wonderful game.

Follow me on Twitter: @comeontheoviedo

Like Johnny Cooper on Facebook:
www.facebook.com/johnnycooperchampionshipmanager

www.chrisdarwen.com

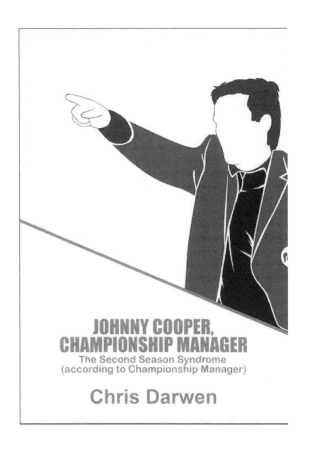

The sequel, "Johnny Cooper, Championship Manager: The Second Season Syndrome" is now available on Amazon.

Foreword

I was first drawn to writing this book in the summer of 2014, having downloaded copies of *Championship Manager '93*, *Championship Manager 2*, *Championship Manager 3*, and *Championship Manager 99/00*. My girlfriend Jess started asking quite a few of the standard "girlfriend" questions that I have encountered over the years, for example, "How can you spend so many hours just watching words on a screen?" If you think about it sensibly, rationally, and take yourself away from our addiction just long enough, you can see it is a very fair question. But that is not the point. A couple of years ago, the excellent book, *Football Manager Stole My Life* by Iain Macintosh, Kenny Millar and Neil White went a really long way to helping people understand what it had been like to be part of the generation that lost months, maybe even years, playing *Champ Man* and then *Football Manager*. But I felt it only scratched the surface of my own addiction. Many times I had gone to bed, wondering where I was going to find that striker that could lead us to promotion, or been sitting on the toilet having an imaginary press conference in my head about our most recent defeat.

Sometimes I would come back from work at lunchtime, just to

get another hour in and then forget to go back to work as I was

worried it would jinx the run we were on. I, and I know many

others, have not just played this game but lived this game in our

heads and it has become real to us. Once I was able to finally

explain this, to Jess, and not my therapist, I realized that I had to

write my own book about it, and that was when Johnny Cooper

was born in my head. I hope you enjoy this book, I really think

that if you are one of the millions that are just like me then there

is lot in here that you will relate to. I think it is important to

point out at this stage, that this is a work of fiction. To actual

people that are mentioned in the book, please take it in the spirit

has been intended, as I am sure you have had a lot worse said in

your real life management careers! Mansfield, for some reason

you will always have a place in my heart, and if anyone can tell

me where Onesimo now lives in Spain, I would love to meet him.

Chris Darwen, September 2nd, 2014.

10-7-99

It's official, it's finally been announced. I, Johnny Cooper, 39, from London Town, have been appointed manager for Mansfield Town FC, the mighty Stags. I'd love to say this is the proudest day of my life, but to be honest I was hoping for the Oxford job. They turned me down. Not too sure about my new boss, the chairman of the Stags, Keith Haslam, or "Hazza" as he prefers to be known. Bit of a farmer, doesn't seem to know much about the beautiful game. I think I might have got the job purely because I played one season on the bench at Forest and he thinks Mr. Clough's magic may have rubbed off on me. Had a look round the stadium, if you can call it that. Hazza reckons it holds 6905 on a good day. Not sure how many of them there have been here, apart from winning the 2nd Division in 1977 apparently. All Hazza and the board expect this season is for us to avoid relegation. "With the football I'm going to bring to Field Mill, Hazza" I say, "This will be the best season of your life!" First game is away to Torquay in a month.

11-7-99

Fuck me that was a tough day. Met the backroom staff today –
Kearnsey, Kev and Bazza. Had to sack the lot of them on the
spot, want my own boys with me, don't I? To be fair, sacking
Kearney was a pleasure, never forgiven him for that tackle he
put in on me in a reserve game up at Gresty Road in '84. Proper
hurt my toe, he did. And Bazza doesn't look like he should be
massaging the boys' legs in my opinion. Got on the blower
straight away to Stace, Richard Stacey. He'll be my number two
as usual. Top lad, great passion in the changing room, clever boy
too, really into all that psychology stuff. Must remember to get
The Independent delivered each day for him, he never takes a
session without reading that over a double espresso. I know,
espresso right? Fucking continental. I prefer a cuppa myself.
Went through the old black book to see who else might crawl out
of the woodwork and fancy a gig here – just won't show them the
training ground, awful facilities.

12-7-99

Got the lads in for a Sunday session, first time I've met them. Barely recognized any of the names on the squad list. Didn't recognize a single face, not one. Well, nearly one – thought we had Andy Linighan until I realized it was his brother, David. Picked on him straight away to lay down a marker, "not even the best player in your family, son," I said. That got a couple of laughs, that. The problem I seem to have here is that the squad is full of wide men, reminds me of a night back home in the West End. I only play this game one way, and it isn't with wingers I tell you! I've got a few days before the Enfield friendly, and this lot are like strangers. Spoke to Hazza about some transfer bunce and he just laughed. Freebies it is then!

14-7-99

Blower hasn't stopped ringing today, thank god I haven't got one of those mobiles, I'd never get any peace. The Field Mill boot room is taking shape, got myself a couple of coaches, which is great news. Brian "Chocky" McClair has come on board as a scout. It means he has forgiven me for smacking him at Plough Lane in '89. I still say it was a bit of handbags. Hopefully Sir Alex has taught him to spot a player – I don't think Sir Alex has ever made a bad signing in his life, he's just bought two top 'keepers for United, that Bosnich could be their number one for the next decade and that Taibi looks top quality. Stace is on board, and Gripper, Dean Gripton, will join me us head scout. Happy days.

15-7-99

Match day! First pre-season friendly against non-league friendly. I spent a lovely few weeks on loan with them back in '85, lovely club. Got to the ground well in advance, helped my new physio, Leathers, hang up the kit for the team. Tell you what, he makes a nice cuppa, might have to make this a bit of a ritual. I reckon he has a few stories. Ah, the smell of the changing room before a match, I've missed this. The team has been picked, going with my usual 4-3-1-2 today. Get it forward, press hard, and keep it tight at the back. Lins is skipper, oldest bloke in the team, right?

No idea how this will go, we haven't exactly looked sharp in training!

Come on! Love that, off to a flyer. 2276 people will go home tonight thinking, "That Johnny Cooper knows what he is doing!" 2-1! Fair play to our loan 'keeper, Muggles, in between the sticks – played a blinder, my man of the match. Tight first half, young Jamie Hudson tapped in from a yard to put us one up at half time. Made four changes at half time, bloody pre-season games, then Big Tone Lormor poached after a great hit by that kid Sisson, or Vidal as I think the lads call him. I prefer Sisso; I'll call him Sisso. They got one back, but we held on. Fish and chips and a bottle of wine for the missus tonight!

19-7-99

Well that has pissed me right off. Frank Clark? Frank Clark?? The most boring man in football only got the job at Oxford. Well, good luck to them. He obviously didn't tell them that Cloughie never rated him as a gaffer, or how he wasted £3.75m on Lee

Bradbury at City – next Alan Shearer he reckoned. Good one, Frank! Off to the North East tonight, Mansfield's idea of a pre-season tour. Great chance for the lads to bond. I hope our Danish coach, Arne, brings his fiddle – apparently he was quite the performer back in Copenhagen. As long as my new goalkeeper coach, Wilko, doesn't start one of his infamous card schools I'll be happy.

20-7-99

Got to love pre-season, right? I don't know why we bothered, in fact half of them didn't! Unprofessional bastards, four of them were in no fit state to play, including my skipper, Lins. Had to get young Craig Disley from the reserves in a taxi and shipped up here pronto. £250 that cost me! Hazza was steaming about it, until Wilko offered to pay it. No idea where he suddenly got £250. Really disappointed in Lins, fined him a week. He shouldn't be setting that kind of example to the young lads like Hudson and Milner – great young lads both of them, but I cannot pick them if they are throwing up in the shower 45 minutes before kick off!

In the end 491 spectators saw Bamber Bridge humble us 2-1, no more than we deserved. Had to hook Kerr and Carruthers at the break, I could smell them sweating lager from the touchline. Danny Bacon begged me to sub him too, but I said, "no Danny, not on your bacon, son." That got a few smirks, that one. I'll pack him off to the reserves when we get back, not impressed. We have another game in two days, we must do better!

22-7-99

Match day! Read the morning papers with Stace in the hotel – saw that Blackburn have signed that little Brazilian, Juninho, for £10m. Lucky Bertie Vogts, getting a new job and £10m to spend within hours. Hazza hasn't given me a tenner! The lads all look knackered before kick off – sober, but knackered. I think Stace might be working them too hard already; I need to review their schedules. Darryl Clarke, Clarkey, is fit though; this might give us a boost.

Goalless draw. That's 90 minutes we'll never get back. They hit the target 11 times according to Arne, he loves a stat that boy. All I know is that our young back up 'keeper Ali "Brimful of" Asher was superb in goal, a proper 10/10 performance tonight. I think Huds was impressed I even understood the nickname, of course I did, I've got all of Cornershop's CDs. Got back to the hotel to be told by Hazza he has cancelled the rest of the tour, we can't afford to stay in the hotel any longer. I manage to convince him to let us stay one more night so the lads can let their hair down. Chocky called me to tell me he has found a Scottish right back to have a look at on trial as he is "an excellent prospect." Turner, my European scout, also called telling me he had found two excellent signings – a Dutch midfielder and an Italian defender.

24-7-99

Woke up to the news that Stoke have received two bids for Muggles. Typical, news of that first friendly must have got out! £170k they reckon, not even going to ask Hazza to try and match it! Also see that Wenger has bought that French lad, Pires. £10m. Crazy money, doubt he'll do anything over here. The League Cup draw was made, we all gathered around the radio at the training ground. You can imagine our delight when Halifax came out of the hat! Jonno called me with a couple of kids he wants me to look at. Both are keepers, might take them both on trial.

25-7-99

Gave myself the day off today, Stace can look after the boys. Decided to get some brownie points in the bag with the missus so I can watch the Copa America Final tonight. Took her out shopping in Mansfield, showed her what a wonderful town this is. I'm not sure she was that impressed to be honest, kept asking when we could go for a day out in the West End. Did enough to watch the Copa America though, Argentina beat Columbia 2-1. Ortega and Batistuta got the goals. That Ortega is some player, could go on to do more than Maradona I reckon. Not sure if he could cut it on a cold, wet Wednesday night at the Mill though.

26-7-99

Woke up early, got a call from Turner telling me that Swansea are also in for Vink, the Dutch midfielder he recommended. I've been to Swansea; it's cold and grey. Sadly, so is Mansfield so I reckon it will come down to the bunce on offer. Offered some more trials to the lads the scouts reckon are excellent prospects.

29-7-99

Training is a bit busy at the moment, triallists everywhere! Muggles is off to Wigan, shame for us – great lad and does a wonderful Jack Dee impression.

1-8-99

Just back from Wembley, watched Arsenal beat United 1-0 in the Charity Shield. Goal on the stroke of half time, by a lad called Graham Barrett. What a talent, if he doesn't play 100 times for Ireland I know nothing!

2-8-99

Not sure if I should be worried, but Hazza just popped into the training ground just to let me know that the "Mansfield Directors are looking forward to a long and successful era under your management." Strange, that. Also heard on the grapevine that one of my old clubs, Forest, are interested in young Milner. I was straight on the blower to Platty, who I have always got on well with since that night in Bari where he showed me and the missus wonderful hospitality after we got lost going for a walk near Basilica di San Nicola. He denied the rumours about Milner.

4-8-99

Turner has come through with a great tip. Found me a Spanish attacking midfielder on a free, Alvaro Cervera. I think cervera is a beer in Spanish; he'll fit in well with Lins and Wilko then! Got a couple of caps for Spain in the late 80's apparently.

6-8-99

Watched the stiffs get a 3-3 draw with Torquay at the Mill tonight. Boulding got a brace and MOM. Wasn't impressed with the lad in goal who is on trial, will let him go. The kid Jervis was superb too, real engine. Told him that if he keeps that up then his dreams of first team football with the Stags will come true sooner than he thinks. Felt like Noel Edmonds after the game, handing out contracts to some deserving young men.

7-8-99

This is the buzz I have missed! Getting up at 3am to get on the coach down to Torquay as Hazza refused to let us have an overnighter. Made sure all the lads were comfy though, most slept all the way down to the South Coast. Got into Torquay at 11am, stopped at Anstey's Cove for a walk along the beachfront to stretch the legs before sitting down for lunch at The Hole in the Wall for our pre-match meal. Told the lads the team, no real surprises as I am sticking with the lads that started most of the friendlies. Got to Plainmoor at 13:30, lads are currently warming up with Stace. Nerves are kicking in, have we done enough to be ready for today? Have we got goals in us? Can we keep it tight at the back?

Fuck me; it's going to be a long season. They battered us. 5-1! 5-1!!! It didn't look particularly good when they went ahead after 2 minutes, but we steadied the ship and kept it tight up until injury time when they scored another two and we got one back. 3-1 down at half time and I have been up since 3am. No point screaming at them, so I stay calm and make a couple of tweaks. They made all the difference as we only lost the second half 2-0. Hazza was straight in my ear after the game, saying the board "were very unhappy with the performance." Yeah, and I am delighted am I, Hazza? It's going to be a long trip home; Arne

can't even bring himself to get the fiddle out.

8-8-99

Wake up in a right mood. Got in at 2am. Phone call from Gripper

at 7am to try and cheer me up, he knows what I am like after a

defeat. Tells me about this excellent prospect he saw yesterday

in the local park leagues. I'll give him a trial. After breakfast I

hear that Cervera has agreed terms and will be with us in the

morning. Got to the training for 11 to debrief the team on

yesterday's shambles and tell them about our new signing.

Clarkey's face fell when I told them what position he plays.

9-8-99

Met Cervera for the first time today. Poor lad only speaks

Spanish, so I left him with Arne and our German coach, Gerhard,

in the hope they can help him settle in. Good session, the lads

are hungry for Halifax tomorrow. I think I have settled on a side.

Blakey in for DK on the right of the midfield 3, Disley comes in at right back.

10-8-99

Nothing like a cup-tie to free me from the stress of the league. I can't abide managers that put out weakened teams in this great competition. You try telling Luton fans that this trophy means nothing after they won it in '88, or Oxford fans after they won it in '86, or Norwich fans after they nicked it in '85! God, I hope the FA Cup never goes the same way. Halifax tonight, they lost at Northampton on Saturday. I can't see anything in their squad to worry us. Got to the ground nice and early, put the kit out with Leathers and had a cuppa with him. He told me a story about the World Cup Semi Final in 1930. Apparently the USA physio ran on the pitch to have a go at the referee. Throwing his bag to the floor in disgust he accidentally opened some chloroform and hit the deck as it knocked him out. As I thought, Leathers loves a story, I hope they improve though. The lads arrive on time, buzzing for the match. Announced the team, Clarkey looked relieved as he keeps his place, Cervera on the bench. Told them I expect a win tonight, no questions.

I'll take that, one each. We could have scored in the first minute; Blakey headed a good chance over. They went one up after 30, but Chrissy G quickly got us level after Blakey played him in. He nearly nailed a worldy on the volley just before half time. Brought Cervera on in the 2nd half, he looked sharp and forced a couple of good saves from their 'keeper. Much better that, should give us some confidence. Shock of the night, Chester beating Wolves 1-0!

11-8-99

Turner's at it again, calling me at the crack of dawn with another tip-off. Another Spaniard, Onesimo. Quick, good off the ball, technique, agile, can dribble. I nearly choke on my Weetabix. He was at Barca for a year under Johan Cryuff, so he will have trained alongside Platini, Koeman and Salinas. I get an offer in straight away; I don't care if I have never seen him play! £475 a week might be a bargain. Preston faxed in an offer of £15k for our young right back, Disley. I was straight on to Moysey to tell him no, firmly. Poor lad that Moysey, he won't be in management long.

↓

12-8-99

Somebody must have seen something I haven't. Another offer for Dizzy, this time from Bournemouth and its £20k. I speak to Wilko and he thinks I should gamble and reject it, see if they are prepared to go to £30k. I could buy 5 cheap Scandinavian talents for that.

13-8-99

Friday the 13th, a good day for the reserves. They beat Hull 4-1, Jervis is superb again. One of the many triallists, Stefan Venetiaan, scored. Offered him a deal. The lad Cunningham was superb in the middle of the park, scored one and set up two. Offered him a deal and he'll be in the first team pretty sharpish. The other highlight was young Andy Vaughan, sweet left foot. He gets a deal as well. I also hear that Vink has signed for Swansea, *quelle surprise* as the Dutch say.

14-8-99

Another early start as we are off to Hull. Grim place, Hull. Can't see them ever being more than a Division Three club. Turner called me to let me know that Kettering are in for Onesimo. I told him not to panic, "If he is the One then it will go fine." I don't think Turns got that one. Judging by our walk along the docks at Hull there are a few tired legs here today might have to rethink my eleven.

Decided to rest Sisso and Milner, and dropped big Tone Lormor. After three minutes I didn't think it was going to make any difference as Lins brought done Featherstone in the area. Penalty, red card, ten men, reshuffle and 1-0 down. I brought on Big Sam's kid, Craig Allardyce, for Blakey and dropped Clarkey into midfield. It looked inspired, as not only did Chrissy G notch the equalizer ten minutes later, he walloped a 35-yard worldy into the top corner to put us ahead! Lads were buzzing at half time, I let Stace bring them back down to earth for the mess leading up to the pen, and then I played good cop telling Chrissy G that City didn't have a clue letting him be here on loan. Second half was backs against the wall, Bowlers making some fine saves. Roscoe had a chance for 3-1, but hit the side netting. We couldn't hold on, their sub Tucker nicked one to make it 2-2. Very proud of the effort today though, first point and I let the lads have a few beers on the coach home.

15-8-99

Hazza has a mobile phone, which I hate. I hate it more as this is how we found out that the FA have banned Lins for 4 matches for that professional foul. What a load of bollocks that is. Is football going to end up being non-contact? I was going to fine him a week, but I can't bring myself to do that now. I saw Dizzy in a right grump on the coach, not having a beer with the lads. Asked him why he was looking so pissed off, and we was upset that I had turned down the Preston bid, reckoned I was treating him unfairly. "Preston, lad? You stay with me and you'll have proper clubs like Bristol Rovers after you in no time!" I don't think he got the joke. It's been reported in the papers that Sir Alex has signed Joao Pinto for £20m. That is proper money, that. I can't see that transfer record ever being broken. Can't see how he will fit into that 442 though, especially with Yorke and Cole starting the season so well again. Turner was on the blower again, Austrian lad this time called Sabitzer. Striker, has played 6 internationals and got a goal. I offer a deal, mad not to! He also mentioned a 20-year-old centre back, might offer him a trial.

17-8-99

The FA are busting my balls, I have just been told I cannot take on anymore triallists as I have no more room in the squad. I bet Barry Fry never suffered from this in his Birmingham days.

18-8-99

The Spanish lad declined the trial anyway. Makes me think he might be quite good, so I send him an offer. Imagine Arsene

Wenger offering a trial to a top European talent? God no, he'd have an offer on the table before you could say Ibrahamovic. So shall I! Turns out Wycombe got there first though, oh well.

19-8-99

Brilliant news, got a call from Turner and he is singing "She's the One" by that Robbie Williams – turns out he did get the joke, and Onesimo will be joining us next week once some of the triallists have left and the FA let me add to the squad. Big game tomorrow, Hartlepool at home. Friday night football, love it. They've won one and lost one so far. Their front two worry me a bit though, and in Gary Strodder they have a unit at the back. Sleepless tonight I reckon.

20-8-99

Only one change tonight, Sisso comes back in to centre mid. Got Stefan "The Blind" Venetiaan on the bench, as well as Carl Cunningham, after they both accepted the offers I put in front of them. Usual cuppa with Leathers after we put the kit out, he was a little quiet though. Nerves I reckon. Lads looked fired up in the warm up.

I can barely write this down, I am furious! Tight first half, 0-0 at the break. Early in the 2nd half Cervera is one on one with the keeper and puts it into orbit. From the goal kick they go straight down the pitch and score. Then they get a second late on, both scored by the front two that I was worried about. To cap it all off, Chrissy G reacts to something their lad says, punches him and gets a straight red. I'm left trying to work out the Spanish for "Next time, just fucking hit it!" Hazza isn't happy, again.

23-8-99

Reserves hammer Hartlepool 5-1 at their place. Didn't go as we are working on not playing a shit offside trap in training. Turns out I might have been wrong on the young 'keeper on trial – MOM last night. Deal on the table for him then! Jervis was class again, first team for him on Saturday. Young Greek triallist called Niklos scored, but I'll wait this time I think. Persuaded

Hazza to let us go to Halifax overnight, cup game, win and we might get a big tie. Will leave tomorrow and make the 68-mile trip in an hour or so. No overnighter for Torquay, four and a bit hours, but overnighter in Halifax. Cheers Hazza.

25-8-99

Told Blakey he was dropped for tonight, and he was far from impressed, shouting the odds and everything. Told him to get the train back to Mansfield, not having that around here disrupting the squad, I'll deal with him tomorrow. "The Blind" starts up front, young Jervis on the bench. Watch out for us defending a bit deeper, could do with a win tonight!

It's getting painful, this. We must take our chances! We had seven shots on target and scored once, according to Arne. They had six and scored three. Furious. Back to the drawing board again. "The Blind" does get his first for the club though, the only plus point.

26-8-99

Onesimo is finally with us; maybe he'll get a few goals for us. Someone needs to! Hopefully his English is so bad that he will not realize we are third bottom and out of the League Cup before the end of August! Brighton on Saturday, they have lost two on the bounce as well.

28-8-99

Throwing Onesy straight in, fuck it, sink or swim! Craig Allardyce comes in for Lins, Gibbo comes into centre mid, just like he did in the Hull game. Haven't heard from the chairman in days. Lads seem quiet in the pre-match meeting, a few nerves kicking in. Stace tries to gee them up, good to see that psychology degree being put to good use. Cuppa with Leathers, he tells me about his Uni days down in Brighton. He got up to a few things, that's for sure. I give them a big team talk, telling them to do this for the fans that are here today.

Well, it's amazing the difference an ex-Barcelona striker and a full house can make! What a day, what a debut. Clarkey put us ahead in the 21st minute, a hopeful hit sneaking in. Then it was the Onesimo show. 26 minutes in he beat 4 men and forced a fingertip save. Then, just after the half hour, he opened his Mansfield account, a fierce shot from 15 yards. 60 seconds later he was at it again, Cervera fed him the ball, he shrugged off one, dribbled past another and took a pot shot. 3-0! I had to sub the lad on the hour, he was dead on his feet and the full house at the Mill showed their full appreciation by giving him a standing ovation. Then, to cap it all off, Clarkey smacked in a half volley with then to go to give us our first win of the season. The dressing room was chaos after the game, all the lads singing and dancing and shouting "Olé!" to everything. Even Hazza was "absolutely delighted," calling us "magnificent." Fish and chips for the missus tonight!

29-8-99

No time to get carried away with celebrations, Cheltenham and Steve Cotterill tomorrow. I've known Steve for years, ever since we were kids at Wimbledon together. He's done a great job with the club, loads of promotions and Dale Watkins is absolutely top class up top. This will be our toughest game yet I reckon.

30-8-99

I hate Bank Holiday matches, the sooner they do away with this one the better. After such a massive win I might need to change it up, centre half Rico and Cervera are still shattered from Saturday. Proper selection dilemma up top now too. Chrissy G and "The Blind" are fit, Big Tone hasn't done much at all but we won on Saturday – plus I have Sabitzer on the bench now as well since he agreed terms. Decisions! I can't jinx it, going with the same 16 that did so well on Saturday. Stace and Leathers agree.

Looks like I got it right! Their star man, Watkins, missed a dubious penalty early on, great save from Bowlers. Proper ding-dong of a first half and they went in one up at the break. Gave the lads as much belief as I could at half time, double sub on 55 minutes and boom! Onesy gave their lad, Griffins, twisted blood beating him three times before hitting another fierce shot into the top corner. Then one of the subs, Sabitzer, hit a howitzer for 2-1! The other sub, young Jonny Milner hit the post and we had them on the ropes! Griffins day got worse as he fouled Rico from a corner and Onesy sent the 'keeper the wrong way. 3-1 and more "Olé's!" in the bath after the match. We are up to 15th now and even Hazza bought a round after the game, saying we'd been "excellent." Going to give the lads two days off to recover before Carlisle away on Saturday.

31-8-99

Player of the Month for Division Three goes to the Cheltenham 'keeper. He wasn't that good yesterday!

1-9-99

Old Bazza is at it again, £25k bid for young midfielder Jonny Milner. Knowing Mr. Fry as I do, I know he loves a haggle so I told him to come back with £100k! Had lunch with the Chairman at The Market Inn, a very simple Scampi and Fries. He told me he is "delighted with the star I have made as manager." We've only won two matches; I do worry about him sometimes.

3-9-99

Bugger me, Barry Fry only came back with the cash! £100k for an 18-year-old kid with 5 minutes experience as a pro. Sold Bazza, sold! I call Gripper, Chocky and Satch in for a scouting meeting. What will £100k get me? I figure at the very least we need a left back, a defensive midfielder and an attacking midfielder/striker.

Chocky rates a lad called Cleeland at Queen of the South, so I fax over a bid of £5k plus 25% sell on. Satch reckons he has a Swedish boy that can play anywhere across the back four, so another bid gets faxed out. Gripper will not shut up about Ged Kielty of Altrincham, so I send him off to watch his next match. Exciting to actually have some cash to spend. Spent the evening watching the reserves draw with Carlisle 1-1. Have to say the kid Jervis impresses me each time. The team have taken the coach up to Carlisle, I do the 4-hour drive later at night. Hazza seems happy to spend on overnighters when we are winning!

4-9-99

The Nottingham Post suggests that Pompey is also in for Milner. Not unless they stump up £100k they're not. I bet Stace didn't find that in *The Independent*. The team looked confident at breakfast, and my only change is going to be handing a first start to Sabitzer "The Howitzer" instead of Big Tone. Clarkey seems a bit tired after a gentle morning warm up, but I cannot afford to rest him.

Wow, what a match – end to end or what? I think it's fair to say we deserved a point. Two down at half time after two great strikes – there is no way Bowlers is stopping either of them! Told the lads to keep believing. 80 minutes in and their sub, Albrighton, tries to do Onesimo over the top, pure filth, reckless challenge. Luckily the ref got it right and sent him off. Then Milner shows me what we will be missing with a class goal, and then sets up "The Blind" to get us level! Injury time could have gone either way, they hit the post and Cunningham forced a wonder save from Weaver that earned him MOM. Three games unbeaten, confidence is growing! Hazza gets a phone call from Gripper, saying that they couldn't see Kielty as he didn't make it off the bench but reckons I should look at Ally Pickering, their 32-year-old defender. England hammered Luxembourg 7-0, great to see Robbie Fowler getting a brace. If he doesn't go on to break Charlton's record I know nothing.

5-9-99

No such thing as a day off, was hoping to get round Sherwood Forest with the missus today. Got a fax first thing saying that the offer for the Swedish defender had been accepted. Sent him an offer of £400 a week. I get a phone call in the middle of dinner from Jonny Milner which means some offers will need to be withdrawn – he was turned down Peterborough and Barry Fry because they won't guarantee him first team football. I would have thought the amount Bazza rotates his squad, nobody is guaranteed! Not happy, this totally screws my plan to invest in the squad.

6-9-99

Quiet day at the club, got a late fax from Sweden – the deal is on, he has agreed terms. We have £1k in the bank, so that's all good. Do I play him at left back or centre back? Lins and Rico have not convinced so far in the middle, and Talls might be happier in midfield instead of left back. Or should I go out and get another centre back?

8-9-99

Back to focusing on the squad I have, not the one I want. Rotherham at home on Saturday. Ronnie Moore is a lower league managerial legend. Not sure what I make of his side, but Leo Fortune-West will be a handful up front. Had Blakey in the office moaning, feels he should be a first team regular. I told him we have lost every game he has played in! Leathers popped in to tell me that Cervera is out for about ten days with a bruised thigh. Chance for Jonny Milner after all then.

9-9-99

The offer for Cleeland has been accepted, except I don't have the money now. Hazza went even more grey spending £1k on the Swede. Turner reckons he has found us a pacey Italian centre back, but I am not convinced this time. I need to decide what to do about Big Tone. He is now 6th choice up front, so I should probably list him, especially as he is on £600 a week. I'll decide after Rotherham.

11-9-99

Match day, love it. I walk down Market Street and the Stags are out in the pubs early, wishing me luck. Luck? I don't need luck, I need £20k to buy Ged Kielty! No change to the routine, kit out with Leathers then a cuppa. He tells me a story about how he was in the changing room when Brian Laws allegedly threw a plate of chicken wings and Ivano Bonetti. Barbeque sauce all over the walls, apparently. Just one change to the side, Milner in for the injured Cervera. The Swede, Askonius, is on the bench.

Well, that little run is over. It doesn't help when you have ten men for 85 minutes. Rico pulled down Leo Fortune-West when he was clean through, and had to go. We competed, but Fortune-West was unplayable and led them to a 3-0 win. Need to pick the lads up quickly, and find a centre back. Hazza collared me in the corridor, steaming at our "capitulation." What game was he watching, we had ten men!

13-9-99

Rushden are in for Ged Kielty. I've sent an offer over just in case we get some money from somewhere. Big Tone goes on the list, just in case it leads to quick funds.

15-9-99

Plymouth away on Saturday. Hazza had to be wrestled into paying for an overnighter – it's a five-hour coach trip Hazza! I heard the other day that he hates spending money so much that even his wife has to pay for her ticket on match day.

17-9-99

Got a surprise fax from Northampton today, bidding £60k for Clarkey. Got me thinking, if they go to £100k then we are on. Got on the blower to Kev over there and gave him the full sales pitch, hopefully he will have bought it! Then, amazingly, Scunny came in with a £85k offer for Big Tone. Sold! Straight on the blower to Rich Taylor at Alty, slapping in a £25k offer for Kielty and £15k for Pickering. Come on Richy, you know it makes sense. Then it was £6k to Aalesund for their centre back, Vattey. Finally, back north of the border to revive the Cleeland deal. Come on!

18-9-99

He's persistent old Barry, I'll give him that. £100k on the table again for Milner. I accepted it. The Vattoy deal looks promising, contract sent over for him. I'd rather be focusing on three points today against Plymouth, not standing by a hotel fax machine. They are down there with us, lost five on the spin. I'd have a tenner on us today, feeling good. I reckon they'll play their loanee from Spurs, McVeigh. Spoke to him a couple of years back, bright lad – if he gets his head right then he could have a long career. Decided to change both full backs today, young Steve Archibald on the left and Asko on the right. Cervera is also fit. Let's hope that Onesy turns it on!

I have no idea how we lost that. We dominated for the first 45, Gibbo put us ahead, Onesy running past them for fun. Their 'keeper had a blinder and somehow we conceded twice in the second half. Everyone is massively deflated. I left it to Wilko and Arne to list the spirits on the long journey home. Beers all round, card school and a day off tomorrow. That leaves us in 20th, we need to get a win soon. Got in at 3am, to a fax from Vattoy saying he wants £4k a week. So do I lad, so do I.

19-9-99

Faxes everywhere on my day off. First, the Clarke deal is off,
they didn't go to £100k. Then, the Lormor deal is done – he is off
to Scunny, good luck to you Big Tone. Milner said no to Barry
Fry again! He won't like that. The Kielty and Cleeland bids were
accepted, so I faxed over personal terms. Fingers crossed!

Got word just before bed that Ged Kielty is a done deal, £25k
plus 25% sell on clause. He'd better make a difference!

21-9-99

Jesus, Barry, take the hint will you? He's back in again for Milner.
At a guess, if you don't offer him first team football he isn't
joining you! Good session today, impressed with the coaching
team, I am seeing some improvements in the player's stats. Only
downside, Onesimo damaged his shoulder dicking about with
Cervera. What is Spanish for "You prat, we need you Saturday!"

22-9-99

Another new face at the club, Marc Cleeland joins us from Queen
of the South for a mere £10k. He should add some steel to the
midfield. Turned up wearing the worst suit I have ever seen,
shiny and green. Looked like he had bought from a market in
Thailand. "Never been there boss," he said. Funny lad. Oh, and
Milner rejected Bazza, again.

25-9-99

Saturday, match day! Nice cooked breakfast, thanks to the
missus for that. Belly, the reserve team manager, was on the
blower telling me how they beat Halifax 6-1 last night. Hope we
can do the same today. Belly reckons some of the lads I have
dropped to the reserves are starting to play well. I decided to
walk to the ground along Market Street, loads of fans out early,
wishing us luck again. Kit out with Leathers, a lovely cuppa too.
He told me this story about when he was at Southampton with
Graeme Souness and they thought they had signed George
Weah's cousin. Brilliant. No Rico today, banned, and Onesy is out

injured. So, it's a recall for Williams and "The Blind." Halifax are bottom, so hopefully we can avenge the cup defeat and deliver today. I tell the lads as much in the team talk.

Yet another missed chance, or chances I guess. 12 shots on target, 1 goal. Their 'keeper wins man of the match. Killer. We were all over them, but we just cannot get it in the net. Young Jonny nearly saved us, hit the bar from 25 yards. Harsh. Stace bollocks the strikers, I'm considering changing my life-long formation, something isn't right. Doubt I will sleep tonight.

26-9-99

Terrible night's sleep, but I have decided to go 442. It works at Highbury, Old Trafford and even White Hart Lane so it can work at Field Mill. Peterborough have faxed again, I've told them £150k now. We'll have a week of drilling the formation, mix the passing up and press in midfield.

2-10-99

Long week this week. Not had a spare moment to write anything down. Milner said no, again. Leaving selection right up to the last minute today. Changing the match day routine, went for a jog to clear my head, had porridge instead of Weetabix. That'll help, along with going 442. Got to the ground, no cuppa with Leathers today, much to his disappointment. Quick chat with Hazza, who says the board are "delighted with the general performance, but concerned with the recent run of defeats." Me too H, along with the 6000 plus that turn up here every other week. I've decided to give the two new lads, GK and Cleeland, the centre of midfield today. Chrissy G is back on the bench. Big rallying team talk today, got them really fired up. I tell them I want a win, but secretly I would be delighted with a point just to stop the rot.

Again, we match them for shots on target! 442 was a disaster, 4-0 down at half time. Lost it with them, went batshit crazy.

Changed it back to 4312 and we win the second half 1-0, Milner with a lovely goal. No time to panic, yet.

5-10-99

Well, still no call from the chairman. Called a few of my managerial peers for some advice. Everyone was nice and positive, if not caught up in their own issues. Got my plan for Darlington on Saturday, this will turn round, starting then!

9-10-99

Had to ignore calls from Grippers all week, I can't think about new signings right now. Reserves win again, 3-0. Might start picking them if we lose again. Changing the formation again, going 4132 today, strengthen the midfield. Kit out with Leathers, then a cuppa. He tells me a funny story about a match in 1991 between Uruguay's two biggest teams, Penarol & Nacional. There was a dust up between Panamean international Dely Valdez and Penarol defender Goncalves. Valdez was Nacional's striker and he was known for wearing gold chains and other jewellery on the pitch. Both players were struggling, as a corner kick was about to take place for Nacional, Goncalves ripped off one of Valdez's gold chains and hid it in his sock. Nobody in the stadium saw it but the TV cameras caught it apparently, and after the game Valdez and the police were waiting for Goncalvez outside the dressing rooms. Goncalvez was arrested but the charges were later dropped as he had returned the chain. Leathers says this is why this derby became known simply as the "golden-chain derby." In the team talk I speak to the lads about conference football. I was lucky enough never to play in it, but I have heard it is ugly. I'd much rather go up than down. They seem to take it on board. Stace gets them equally fired up in the warm up. Let's go! Darlo are in 12th, but who cares?

Finally! Finally! We were superb today; from the first whistle to the last, all of them, every one of them. Bowlers was incredible in goal, Dizzy looked better than Lee Dixon on creatine at right back, Onesimo was majestic and Ged Kielty looked like a young

Bryan Robson. GK put us one up after Onesy's shot was saved then Chrissy G netted from Onesy's pinpoint cross, a dream first half. The second half was even better; having already hit the post the Spanish matador whacked home a free kick from quite a distance. 3-0! Up to 19th! Hazza was "delighted." Fish and chips for the missus tonight!

13-10-99

Wednesday, and still buzzing following that win. Barnet away on Saturday, last time we played bottom of the league we got beat though. Bazza was on the blower again, £150k for Jonny. "£200k now, Bazza," I said, "He was absolutely class on Saturday!" Need to sit down with the scouts again if he does go, we really need to strengthen.

15-10-99

Just about to leave on the coach down to North London when Bazza calls me and agrees to £200k. I bet Wilko that Jonny still says no. The lads get to choose the music on the way down; I quite like that Eminem fella that they were playing. "The Real Slim Shady", he says. Message for us by the time we get to the hotel, reserves won again, 3-1.

16-10-99

So Underhill, what do you have for us? We've got an unchanged eleven for you, make no mistake. Everyone fit and raring to go, changing room is buzzing. Wilko is very quiet though, apparently Chrissy G took him for a ton in the card school on the way down. Come on boys, three points please!

This game is bad for my health. Two great chances in the first five minutes, both saved by their 'keeper. Then Barnet hit us where it hurts with their first attack. We batter them and batter them and eventually Onesy beats three men and slots home for 1-1. We dominate the second half, but their sub, King, scores with his first touch. There was me watching him warm up thinking, "We'll be ok if he comes on, touch of a criminal that lad." Thank God for GK, as he pops up in the 93rd minute to get us a point. One point gained, or two dropped I ponder. The directors, according to Hazza, were "pleased" though.

17-10-99

A couple of sackings have come through today, first of the season. Colin Lee at Wolves has gone, and that pain in the backside Neil Warnock has been given the chop at Bury. I guess the merry-go-round starts now. I hope Hazza doesn't start getting any ideas! Northampton fax over a £60k bid for Blakey – sold! Got the lads down to the local pub for the FA Cup draw. I'm praying for an easy home tie. I got the second best thing, my boyhood team, Luton Town, will be coming to Field Mill – good crowd for that I reckon.

19-10-99

Birthday today, and all I want is fish and chips with the missus following three points. To earn that, we need three points off Exeter at the Mill tonight. Grateful to still have my job after hearing that Warren Joyce has quit Hull last night. All the lads report in early, Onesy and Cleeland look a little jaded. Going to have to ask them to push through, though, and I will sub them early if the job is done. Kit out with Leathers, cuppa as usual and a bit of birthday cake – top man! He tells me a story about a game he went to watch in Uruguay back in '96. This happened during a Penarol-Danubio game he reckons. Penarol fans were upset at the fact that their team was down 1-0 and with few minutes remaining the fans began throwing all sorts of objects into the pitch, rocks, bottles and the like but what finally caused the ref to suspend the game was the sight of the linesman down, a motorcycle helmet next to him: it had just hit him. A motorcycle helmet! I know, hilarious. "Fucking linesman," Leathers says.

Crazy game, we threw away Onesy's personal two-goal lead, hit the post twice and end up drawing 2-2. No fish and chips tonight, but will be doing some shopping tomorrow for a new centre back.

20-10-99

I find myself putting in bids for two centre backs before lunch.
Going to give Lins a final chance on Saturday, maybe I have been
too harsh. Blakey is off to Northampton, thank god, and my bid
for Preston's Ryan Kidd was accepted before the ink was dry on
the fax – should I be concerned?

21-10-99

In the fastest deal ever, Moysey almost offered to drive him to
me personally, Ryan Kidd joins us for £20k and takes quite a pay
cut. I decide to change my mind on Lins and tell him and Rico
they are free to leave. I need to get this defence sorted. Huge
game on Saturday, away to Barry Fry and Peterborough. We'll
be travelling without Cleeland who has picked up a knock in
training.

23-10-99

Morning coach down to Peterborough. Lins is off to Hartlepool for a medical and agree terms on a free. Onesy looks shattered, and I am also tempted to leave Milner out today after all the Peterborough transfer malarkey. Either that or he might show Mr. Fry exactly why he is worth guaranteed first team football! I expect I will start them both.

I haven't been this proud since my cat, Felix (named after the 1970 Brazil 'keeper) brought me his first mouse on my 7th birthday. We just did Barry Fry at his place, 4-0. Yep, 4-0. Bloody brilliant, we were. Onesy netted a 20-yard free kick to set us on the way, and then Chrissy G got a brilliant second before the onslaught. Bowlers was incredible, saving everything that came his way. Then their centre half totally loses it and puts the nut on Clarkey! Straight red. We dominate from that moment, GK puts a bullet header home from Craigy's corner for three and we go into half time already out of sight. I rest Onesy at the break, "The Blind" comes on and causes all manner of problems before Chrissy G nets his second and our fourth, and the lad nearly got a hat trick too! Happy days, and we are all singing along to Arne on the fiddle on the way home. Chuffed, I am. Bring on Luton next week!

24-10-99

I wake up to the news that Barnet have sacked John Still and Bury have appointed Glenn Hoddle! I guess you are being punished for a past life, Glenn eh? Feel top of the world this morning, feeling very positive of causing an upset against Luton.

25-10-99

I'm having fun with Bazza now, another £200k bid faxed in this morning. "£200k Bazza? Are you mad?" I say, "you saw him on Saturday, £300k probably isn't going to get him now!" Wolves have appointed the former French international, Jean Tigana.

28-10-99

Bloody hell, the big names are prepared to drop down the divisions to get work! Roy Evans at Hull? I can't see him getting the Spice Boys to join him there. Whatever next, Sven Goran Eriksson at Notts County?

29-10-99

Just one injury for the cup-tie tomorrow, "The Blind" is out with a damaged shoulder. Lins is getting plenty of free transfer interest, and Ronnie Moore has just offered me £40k for Rico. Sold!

30-10-99

This is what I went into management for, a shot at the FA Cup. I didn't make the Dons squad back in '88 and it still kills me now. It's even better that it is against the team I grew up following, Luton Town. What a history they have as a club. Steve Foster, Brian Horton, Rade Antic, David Pleat's crazy little jig at Maine Road, Brian Stein, Ricky Hill, Mick Harford. Slightly different nowadays, the wise old sage that is Lennie Lawrence is in charge. It'll be good to see my old mate, Clive Goodyear, though. We were at Wimbledon together. They are 8th in Division Two currently, clear favourites. But who knows, hey? Got down to the Mill early, want to take in the atmosphere. Kit out and cuppa with Leathers who told me a great FA Cup story from the qualifying rounds a few years back. Apparently this young lad, on debut, came on as sub and straight away the ref was on at him for having the wrong colour cycling shorts. The lad protested that he didn't have any, but the ref was having none of it, making him go off and change. The player returned, having to go commando. When the ref asked him to prove that he didn't have shorts pulled up underneath, the young lad dropped his shorts to prove himself, giving the ref and the crowd an eyeful of his crown jewels. The ref sent him off for indecent exposure! Brilliant, I hope that doesn't happen today, we need all the help we can get to beat this lot. Same starting eleven as last weekend, I tell the boys anything could happen today if we can frustrate them or even score early. Full house expected today, so hopefully we can give them something to cheer about!

It might have been completely different if Jonny has slotted it home. A classic "Milner must score" moment in the fourth minute, but he hit it tamely at their 'keeper and thirty seconds later it's in the back of our net. They were clinical, five shots on target resulting in three goals. We had six shots on target, one goal. I took the front three off to rest them when it was clear the game was gone, we didn't deserve to lose that 3-1. Back to the league! Fair play to the fans, standing ovation – they saw the effort the lads put in. Need to get the heads up quickly, Southend come here on Tuesday.

31-10-99

Chairmen are a strange breed. Halifax have sacked Mark Lillis after they beat Alty in the first round of the cup. Harsh on the guy, I found him good company in the three games we have had so far this season. Mind you, they did beat us twice.

1-11-99

Rico has left for Rotherham, good pro that lad. Not so professional is young Gibbo who was late for training and showing a distinct lack of match fitness. Fined him a week and told him how disappointed I was, especially with a big match against Southend tomorrow.

2-11-99

I had a nice confidence boost before the game, lunch with Hazza at the Market Inn, scampi and fries all round. He said the board are "delighted with my performance." Satch belled me with an attacking midfielder he reckons could be an excellent signing. Norwegian boy, could get him for under £10k. Gibbo has been moaning about his fine, apparently, saying it was "unfair." I'll deal with that tomorrow. Might have to freshen it up tonight, Gibbo is dropped so might have to risk Cleeland in his pace, or maybe Cunningham. Milner and Clarkey could do with a rest so I might recall Roscoe and Cervera and put Sisso back on the bench. I'll speak to Stace, see what he thinks. Got to the ground early, decided to add a coat to the match day suit as the forecast is drizzle and only 6 °C. Cuppa with Leathers, who was very quiet tonight, hope he is ok. Decided to freshen it up, so Roscoe, Cervera and Cunningham all start. Southend are 7th, lost in the Cup at the weekend but have a beast of a lad in the middle of the park called Damien Francis. I might stick Cunningham on him. I ask 18-year-old Craig Disley to skipper the side for the first time.

Football can be a cruel, cruel mistress, toying with your emotions. They bombard us in the first 45; we are lucky to go in only one behind. We are still in it though, and it turned out were very in it as Onesimo blasted home a free kick for 1-1. Ten minutes later he hits the bar! Chrissy G was quiet, so I replaced him with Sisso and pushed Cervera up to top with Onesy. It nearly worked, as Sisso played in Roscoe who found the net but was adjudged to have strayed offside. Obviously they went straight up the other end and scored the winner. Fine lines, fine lines. That drops us back to 19th in the table with Macclesfield away on Saturday and they are 20th.

4-11-99

Brian Kidd at Barnet? I really do hope Hazza isn't getting any ideas seeing that Gullit, Hiddink, Zemen, Billardo, Menotti, Kinnear, Domenech, Magath and Venables are all looking for work. I'll try not to think about it. Satch has suggested a Ghanaian striker that we might be able to get on loan. Nothing ventured nothing gained, so I fax over the bid. He also likes this lad called Jethro, half Swede, and half English. Quick, creative and great teamwork. Got to say, I am tempted if only for the name! Might be time for that shopping spree, keep things moving forwards.

5-11-99

The reserves march on, 3-0 winners versus Macclesfield. Jervis, Jones and Boulding bossed it, should I consider them for the first team or keep trying to find bargains in the transfer market? I've had an offer for a 17-year-old centre back, Jardler, and the bid for Jethro accepted. Personal terms faxed over.

6-11-99

8am coach to Macclesfield today, Hazza remaining consistent on no overnighters if we have lost. Switching it back today, Milner, Clarkey and Cleeland all return. A big three points on offer here today. Risking Dizzy and Allardyce even though they are both knackered. Can't imagine Craig's old man ever asking for a rest.

Two points dropped, that. GK found space midway through the first half to put us ahead and we started to play some really nice stuff. Just as I am thinking, "We need a second," they equalize, but straight from kick off Onesy gets fouled 30 yards out, gets up and bam! Free kick, top corner, 2-1! I tell the lads at half time that we are by far the better side and mustn't switch off. After an hour I pull Dizzy off for Asko as he is getting roasted, then the Swede immediately gives away a stupid penalty. 2-2. The lads are gutted, and Asko is beside himself. I ask Arne to tell him, "We all make mistakes, just don't make anymore!" in Swedish. That point keeps us in 19th. I get home to a fax saying that the 17-year-old centre back wants £1k a week. Don't we all, lad. I may switch my attention to a Chilean-Swede that Mullen has found kicking about in South America, as well as a midfielder with 23 caps for Chile.

7-11-99

The loan deal for the Ghanaian is off, as we cannot afford 100% of his wages. I don't think Jethro will be coming either; he wants £5k a week!

8-11-99

So, the bid for the Chilean international, Moises, has been accepted. Considering a 17-year-old wanted a grand a week, I am not feeling too confident about getting this lad on £500 a week. Early conversations confirm this, as his agent wants £7k every seven days. Not likely! Not sure why we didn't scout South America sooner though, seems to be some bargains available if they can get work permits and accept some sensible wages. Training is focused on corner routines this week; I want us actually scoring from some. ↓

11-11-99

I've found that most of my time this week has been spent bidding

on South American internationals. Chilean, Peruvian, Bolivian, I

don't care. One of them must want to come and play for me!

We've already picked up one, a defender, on a free. Hopefully

that will open the floodgates, I reckon I can afford three.

12-11-99

The next lad I speak to wants £7k a week. This does not bode

well! "The Blind" is injured again, he will miss Chester

tomorrow.

13-11-99

I start the day by offering two more contracts that will probably

get laughed at. £100 a week in Peru or £500 a week in lovely

Nottinghamshire? I know what I'd choose. I need to get the boys

up for today; they have been looking a bit down and tired.

Cuppa with Leathers and he has another classic South American story for me, one of the most famous Uruguayan derbies ever, he reckons. It happened in the 1930's and after a Nacional player had hit a ball out of bounds close to the post, the ball returned back to the field thanks to a cameraman's briefcase which was left there, another Nacional player then calmly pushed it in. The referee who was standing far away though the ball had hit the post. This derby became known as "briefcase derby." Those crazy South American's and their catchy nicknames, right? I decide to keep faith with the same 11 despite the temptation to pick Cisternas at left back.

Thank god for Onesimo, that's all I can say – and also thank him for Ian Bowling whilst you are there. One puts them in at one end; the other keeps them out at the other. Six minutes in and Dizzy puts Onesy in behind. The Spaniard sprints in and scored with a low right-footed drive. Ten minutes later, yet another free kick is given to us and a superb effort from the main man flies in again. We get to half time two goals to the good and the chat is about keeping it tight and how the next twenty minutes will decide this game. They absolutely hammer us second half, Bowler stopping all but one effort, which gave us a very nervy final fifteen minutes. Three points though, fish and chips with the missus tonight! Twenty points on the board and up to the heady heights of 17th.

14-11-99

Spent the day telling South Americans I'm not able to pay them £7k a week. Got a rare Saturday off next weekend so will give the boys a couple of days off this week. Away to Rochdale a week Tuesday.

20-11-99

I, like plenty of others, was gripped by the England-Russia play off tonight. Russia were through on away goals with 7 minutes to go before Andy Cole came off the bench to grab the decisive equaliser on the night and the winner overall. This is the player that Glenn Hoddle, when he was still England manager, said needed five chances to score one goal. Two things here. Firstly,

Glenn, that is why you are now manager of Bury and Coley is scoring for fun at Manchester United. Secondly, I'd love another striker that scores one in every five chances. Curiously, Scotland sneaked through on penalties and still sacked Craig Brown. No doubt we will see him soon in the 2nd or 3rd Division. Matty Mullen keeps sending me incredible South American players to consider, one of them will take £500 a week. I might consider releasing some reserves to get the wage bill down.

23-11-99

Daytime coach trip to Spotdale, no point going overnight, keep that one in the bank. Cervera, Cunningham and Gibbo all stayed at home due to injury. The lads all turned up wearing sombreros as they heard about me scouring the South American market. Arne is confused; he thinks the sombrero comes from Mexico. I make a note to start scouting Mexico; maybe they take £500 a week. Same starting eleven, I tell the lads to think back to Peterborough, our last away win. The boys seem jaded; I make another note to get Spence to take it easier in training. I hope they have enough in the tank for tonight.

It's rare I think we have been lucky to get a point! Another MOM for Bowler, that tells me a lot. The back four were fast asleep for the first half, hooked Allardyce at half time and Dizzy early in the second as their legs and heads had gone. Luckily we recovered from 2-0 down as a worldy from Onesy and a tap in from Chrissy G got us level. They had 20 shots on target, yet we nearly nicked it when Clarkey was blocked from four yards. I'll take that point, thank you.

24-11-99

Another one bites the dust, Holloway's been sacked at Bristol Rovers. Lovely man Ian, I know how much he loves that club. We were at Wimbledon together, briefly, in his terrible year there. He just wanted to be in Bristol, poor guy.

25-11-99

Had to pull half the lads out of training today, they are looking totally wiped out. Need to monitor this more closely, as if I don't have enough to do. December is going to be a hard month, need them fit. Northampton on Saturday, here at the Mill. Big, strong, powerful side.

27-11-99

Match day! Hammering it down so I drive to the club. I've decided to rest Jonny Milner, but the rest seem to be fresher after a rest. Cisternas comes in at left back and I push Tallon up into midfield. Cuppa with Leathers, he is on top form but no time for stories today.

Another fucking opposition goalkeeper gets MOM here, and for the first time this season, amazingly, I am spitting feathers at the referee. Stace had to pull me away from his room and the end. Never a fucking penalty, they both jumped with their arms up so how can he fucking give that? They scored early and sat back, so we dominated the first half but couldn't get level. Skipper Clarkey, possibly sensing he is on my hit list, equalised with a great header before that fucking idiot cheated us out of a point. Nice to see Lins and Blakey back at the club, I reminded them that was the first time they had won here this season. Fuck knows how they are 5th and we are 18th.

30-11-99

My old Wimbledon gaffer, Harry Bassett, has been given the boot by Barnsley. I have to call the scouts and tell them firmly to stop sending me excellent prospects for the future. I need excellent signings, now! York away on Saturday, they are 4th. Somehow, we are only a good run away from the play-offs.

1-12-99

Surprise, surprise, Craig Brown comes in at Bristol Rovers. Sadly, we say goodbye to Chrissy G today as his trial period has ended and he is back up to Manchester City, hopefully more experienced for his time here. Might look into the reserves for his replacement. Hazza assures me he hasn't been speaking to El Tel, or Joe Kinnear, or Ian Holloway and that I am being paranoid as he and the directors are still "delighted." Easily pleased it would appear.

4-12-99

Strangely nervous today. Apprehensive about our chances. The lads are relaxed focused and ready though, so it's the same 11 apart from "The Blind" coming in for Chrissy G. This is definitely a chance for someone to start scoring goals alongside Onesy. We have nothing to lose today, most expect us to get battered and that probably includes me!

It certainly felt like it was going to be another one of those days when "The Blind" and Clarkey missed sitters in the first 20 minutes. Then Onesy, as ever, beat their lad to Dizzy's corner and scored – nice to see that practise paying off! We were bossing it, which of course meant they must be about to equalise, which of course they did. One shot, one goal for them in the first half, too familiar. Luckily we didn't let up in the second half and Talls was clipped having made a break into their area. The whole bench leapt up at the same time, shouting, "PENALTY!" and we actually got it! Onesy, keeper wrong way, 2-1 and a very pleasing three points! Hazza was happier than ever on the coach home, "absolutely delighted" and "magnificent" he kept saying. We have the Autoglass Trophy on Wednesday, Chesterfield at home – I'm not sure if it is a welcome distraction or not, but it's another road to Wembley!

7-12-99

And this is why we invest in our scouting here at Mansfield. Turner has found me the perfect partner for Onesimo. A 19-year-old Cameroon/French boy playing in the Spanish regionals. Eight in thirteen this season and he's got power, pace, long shots, stamina and finishing. The bid has gone in, I want him, I want him quite a lot. I'm bouncing to the ground, but that soon changes when Onesy asks if he can rest tonight. He is only 80% he tells me, in terrible English. Tough dilemma, this. Onesy at

80% is still better than most at this level at 100%. This is another shot at Wembley, but I also need him for the weekend. I tell him to win it for us in thirty minutes, then I'll sub him and he can go back to Spain for a few days and see his family. Other than that it is totally the same approach as against York. Cuppa with Leathers, but he is very quiet, nerves I hope.

What a match, played in front of the smallest crowd of the season. The 4500 that stayed at home certainly missed out! We come in at halftime one down, but they are down to ten after their right back fouled Onesy one time too many. Onesy begs to come off at half time, but I tell him ten more minutes and then, if we win, he can go straight to the airport. Ten minutes pass and nothing happens, so I gamble and bring on all three subs. Straight away they break from our corner and go two up. Game over. Their 'keeper, Tyler, is stopping everything that comes his way, amazing performance, but eventually Sisso beats him with just fifteen left on the watch. Deep into injury time Sisso crosses and "The Blind" heads it goal wards, forcing yet another wonder save from Tyler – but the rebound falls to Sabitzer "The Howitzer" who scores from 10 yards out to force extra time! Extra time had to be ours, they were done. Sure enough, Milner crossed and Venetiaan scored the first golden goal in Mansfield's history! Wembley is one step closer. I felt for their lad Tyler, who'd been amazing. I shook his hand and told him Bazza had let a good one go again. Our only downside was Cleeland getting another yellow, meaning he misses a game. Hazza bought a round for the second time this season, "absolutely delighted" and "magnificent" are becoming his favourite words!

8-12-99

I decided to give a few of the more tired legs the rest of the week off. A couple of them decided to go to Spain with Onesimo, which is great team togetherness. I have the feeling I'll be spending the rest of the week dreaming of a Cameroonian striker.

9-12-99

I get a call from Stace, telling me we have got Wrexham at home in the Autoglass, 11th Jan.

11-12-99

I woke up to the news that the reserves won again, 1-0 down in Swansea. A good omen for us today? It's the first time we have played top of the league. I catch Onesy in the gym before the team meeting, and he just about manages to tell me that he is "100% ready." Leathers was on good form over our cuppa, telling me about how Liam Daish got a ban at Birmingham for playing a toy trumpet one of the fans had thrown in the pitch. Ref booked him, and it took him over 41 points! I consider putting in my programme notes next week a plea to the fans not to throw toy instruments on to the pitch, just in case. Same starting eleven today, Sisso, Milner and Sabitzer were all brilliant off the bench in the week but my heart says go with the same eleven.

Value for money that match, a proper ding-dong! They get an early lead, some South American defending at the back post from Cisto gives them a penalty, and they convert. Then goals were exchanged within two minutes of each other, GK getting his first for a while. The stroke of half-time brought another exchange of two goals, ours another great free kick from Onesy. 3-2 down at halftime. I decide to save Cisto from himself and bring on Milner in his place. Their bargain buy from Swansea, Morah, got his second for 4-2, so I throw Sisso and "The Howitzer" into the fray and boom! Two huge headers from the Austrian and we come away with a 4-4 draw and an unexpected point! My nerves are gone, and that result puts up to eleventh, our highest place yet. We've scored forty goals now, just two less than Swansea who are still top, but we have let in forty one, which is just two fewer than Hull who are bottom!

12-12-99

The news I have been waiting for, Lorca have accepted my offer for the striker. Quite worried that his agent is going to price his wages out my range though.

15-12-99

Quiet week, one deal for a Brazilian collapsed due to a work permit issue. Got to decide whether to give Sisso and Milner a run alongside GK in midfield, they've been doing brilliantly off the bench. Shrewsbury away on Saturday.

17-12-99

The Cameroon boy rejected the contract. Disappointing. I think agents are becoming a curse. Off to Shrewsbury on the coach now.

18-12-99

Nice hotel this. Stayed up late with the backroom boys, great night talking about the future, the lads, the past, everything really. I have the rare treat of a fully fit squad to choose from. Just one change, "The Howitzer" comes in for "The Blind." Sisso and Milner can wait; Cisto gets another chance at left back.

It was very strange to see my old mate Vincent Jones lining up for the Shrews. Hell of a fight today, Kidder got his first goal for us before disaster struck and Cleeland went all Vinnie Jones. Two footed challenges seem to result in red cards this season, and seventy minutes is a long time to play with ten men. They scored twice to go in 2-1 up. I shuffled the pack at half-time, Dizzy off, three at the back, Sisso on. He rewarded me instantly, by setting up Clarkey for 2-2 and then putting us ahead! Bowler was then lucky to stay on the pitch, cleaning out their striker for a pen. 3-3, and I'm happy to take that with ten men away from home. Three at the back was interesting; maybe I could do that and get another striker involved. I tell Cleeland that red will cost him a week's wages. He takes it like a man, no whinging about this kid.

22-12-99

Christmas is coming, so Lincoln decide to sack John Reames. I'm going to try the new formation against Lincoln on Boxing Day. I'll keep Dizzy on the bench just in case I need to change it back to a back four.

25-12-99

Christmas Day, always a funny one when you are involved in professional football one. Dinner is always a rushed affair, as we have to train in the morning and then watch what we are eating in the afternoon and evening. Well I don't anymore, but the players do. I watched the Queens speech where she talked about moving from one millennium to another, and then the Christmas Day film, *Jumanji*, starring that genius, Robin Williams. That just about kept my mind off Lincoln long enough!

26-12-99

There is something about Boxing Day matches that excites me. It's a different atmosphere, I think after a day of being trapped with the family a lot of people are delighted to have somewhere to escape to. I'm delighted we are at the Mill today; it meant the lads did get some family time yesterday. Kit out and a cuppa with Leathers. He tells me a great story about this game he played in as a kid, a Cambridgeshire league match that was played one winter in typically murky conditions. After about 10 minutes, the fog came down so thickly that visibility was reduced to about half the length of the pitch, so the referee decided to abandon the game. It was only after Leathers and the players had been enjoying the warmth of the changing rooms for about 20 minutes that a player on team noticed that their goalkeeper had not come in. When they went out to look for him they discovered him still faithfully guarding his goal, oblivious to the fact that the match had been abandoned. Apparently, he thought his team had been playing particularly well and had managed to keep the play at the other end of the pitch... Brilliant! I'm going three at the back today. Stace thinks I have had too much brandy at the Christmas lunch, Wilko bets me a score that we will lose by three, Leathers says that if he had known I was serious he wouldn't have made me a cuppa. So Clarkey pushes up top, Sisso starts and Gibbo comes back in to anchor the midfield in the Nobby Stiles role.

Well that's £20 Wilko owes me! Happy bloody Christmas! I love a 4-0 win, we totally bossed that. Kidder scored from a set piece, two more from Onesimo and then Clarkey rounded it off by giving it the full Keith Houchen for number four. I was able to rest a few after an hour as we have a hectic few days ahead. We are still 16th, and we finally have a positive goal difference! I have never seen Hazza so happy. Torquay come here in three days, revenge boys, revenge!

29-12-99

The games are certainly coming thick and fast now, Torquay here tonight. They are third. I am going to go with the same line up as against Lincoln. Cardiff have sacked Frank Burrows and Lincoln have gone with Neil Warnock, bet he was glad to have missed the game against us. El Tel's has gone to Woking of all places. Leathers rules out Milner for tonight, bruised ribs. I over-rule him and keep him on the bench, no cuppa for me! Come on lads, same again!

Oh it feels good, it feels good. A dominant 3-1 win. Onesy sent us on the way from the spot; Clarkey doubled it after a great run from deep. I brought on Cervera and he crossed for GK to make it three! They got a late consolation, but who cares. After the celebrations they had at Plainmoor after doing us 5-1, they can enjoy their coach ride home. Come on! Hazza has his hand in his pocket again. "Becoming a habit this, Hazza!" I say. All he can say in reply is "Excellent, excellent!" This was the last game of the millennium at Field Mill, what a way to finish 1999.↓

30-12-99

The last bit of business has been done for '99. Gary Tallon tells me he is leaving on a Bosman at the end of the season. I make some gag about the Millennium bug getting us all and none of us will be here on Saturday, let alone next June. He laughs, and then promises me that he will do all he can to get us promoted this season. Promoted? The thought hadn't really crossed my mind, but actually, it is on!

3-1-00

So, as Jarvis Cocker once sang, "Let's all meet up in the year 2000!" Some of the lads understood that one, but more importantly, everything still works! I let the lads have a quiet Millennium Party, and I think they respected my wishes for no repeats of the pre-season tour. They all looked fine in training. Bottom of the table Hull are coming to the Mill today. The last time I saw Roy Evans he was giving me dogs abuse at Anfield when we were there with the Dons. I haven't forgotten that. Three points today will help ease the pain, though. There is a bit of sleet out there, and it's -1 apparently, might go for a scarf as well as the coat. Onesy turned up dressed for the Arctic Circle, Wilko gave him absolute pelters. To be fair to Onesy, he just smiled and said, "I score 20 in 20." Fair point, Onesy lad. The squad is fully fit, so I ask them for the same as the last performance. No cuppa with Leathers today, as he hasn't turned up – strange, that.

I think Wilko must have upset Onesy a little bit, suggesting he didn't fancy it, as it was cold out there. Onesimo 3, Hull City 0. Right foot curler, penalty, beat four players and thump it home. Gorgeous, what a beautiful, beautiful player. I couldn't resist a dig at Evans after the game, asking if he'd had an invite to the Liverpool Christmas Party, just to remind him what football used to be like for him. We are up to 12th after that, just four points short of the play-offs. Unbeaten in seven, three wins on the bounce and I appear to have a new best mate in Hazza.

5-1-00

The first sacking of the new Millennium, one of the best players of the previous one, Bryan Robson has gone from Middlesbrough. He only rebuilt that club and their reputation, right? Brian Flynn, one of the nicest men in the game, has also gone from Wrexham. We've got them in the Autoglass next week. Chocky reckons he has found me a match winner. The lad Aitken from Queen of the South looks very promising; he has ten goals from midfield this season. I am going to watch United on TV this evening; they are down in Brazil for the FIFA World Club Championship. It has been quite controversial them missing the FA Cup to play in this tournament, another sign that football is changing.

United's mix of reserves and first eleven cruised past Raja Casablanca, 2-0. I am sure there must be tougher sides to play than them. Rumours have also started that Zidane maybe leaving Juventus for AC Milan, £15m it is reckoned.

7-1-00

The proper Manchester United XI beat the South American champions, Vasco, 1-0 tonight. Fabio Cannavaro and Jaap Stam were immense at the back for United. We're off on the coach to Hartlepool, can the run continue?

8-1-00

It's cold and wet in Hartlepool today. Had a good chat with Leathers this morning, checking in that he is ok after his no show earlier in the week. It turns out that his wife threw him out over Christmas, she has been having an affair with an old teammate of his – and it's been going on for a decade. No wonder the guy has been a little bit up and down. Stace looks up from *The Independent* and offers him a room at his place, nice one Stace. The boys are buzzing for this one; they want four on the bounce. I go for the same eleven again, and it's our first time playing three at the back away from home.

Oh my! Something special is clicking into place right here, right now. To come up to Hartlepool and leave with all three points is very, very promising. Onesy got both in the first half, one was even a header, and he very nearly turned it into another hat trick but his pile driver hit the bar. They pulled one back, but the lads dug in and we settled it through a third goal, scored by "The Blind." The vibe has definitely changed in the changing room;

these boys are starting to feel like they can do something. I reckon we are one big centre back and another pacey striker away from doing something incredible, it isn't totally unthinkable to look at the top three spots. Hazza is beside himself, "9th! 9th! Magnificent!"

10-1-00

What a few days it has been, I've hardly had time to take it all in. I'm thinking about finding those two players as a priority, and put it in tentative bid for a Gambian striker that fits the profile I am looking for. Brian Little has left WBA for Middlesbrough. Real Madrid beat United in the Maracana tonight. I couldn't understand Sir Alex's selection, it was almost as if he wasn't bothered. Wrexham tomorrow, huge cup-tie that I am very bothered about.

11-1-00

Match day! I start the day learning that the kid Aitken wants £3k a week. Next! GK has a slight knock according to Leathers. I am going to have to risk upsetting him, again, by playing GK anyway. Cleeland is back in for Gibbo. God, I want to win this one. The boys are ready; there is a real look in their eyes.

I have no idea how we lost that, we are superb tonight. Nineteen shots on goal, but they were going everywhere except the back of the net. I cannot explain it, gutted is not the word. Maybe Stace has a better word. I cannot even bring myself to describe the game; another shot at Wembley has been taken away from me. We have a long trip down to Brighton at the weekend; we must get back on track.

13-1-00

I might have just found a lad from AFC Bournemouth that is a deadly finisher. Kidder is out for a month, picked it up in training. That is a worry.

15-1-00

United finished third in Brazil. I would class that as poor. Madrid were allowed to win it without even breaking sweat. The deal of Jorgenson is done; he will join us from Bournemouth in time for kick off. I might stick him on the bench. Asko is coming in for Kidder today; I'm also resting GK so Jonny Milner starts. Gibbo comes back in for Cleeland.

Well, there is no need to press panic just yet. Onesy gave us a dream start, but we conceded two shockers to cost us three points. I am worried about the defence without Kidder. Another long coach trip home!

19-1-00

So Zidane did go to AC Milan after all, effigies of him were being burned in Turin overnight. I had a sleepless night trying to work out what to do about our defence, Asko really worries me. Lennie Lawrence has left Luton to go to WBA. I'd love that job, one day. A freebie Thai striker tempts me, it is claimed he has 15 goals in 23 internationals. Is he worth a gamble? At £90 a week, quite possibly!

22-1-00

We have Cheltenham away, today. No overnighter, thanks
Hazza, so an early start to make the two and a half hour coach
journey. Talls didn't make it as far as the coach as he has picked
up an injured ankle. Jonny Milner starts, GK is back and I am
going to experiment with Dizzy in the back three. This will tell
me a lot about our character. Wilko reckons we are going to
lose, Stace says draw and Leathers is backing a win.

Fuck me, we were awful today. Absolute rubbish. There was an
early let off when they hit the bar, but did we learn? We fell
behind two minutes later. Absolutely nothing was happening for
us until we finally got the ball to Onesy – he beats three men and
scores. Simple! The second half was worse though, they score
early. I sent Jorgy on off the bench, and he nets a clinical
equaliser, then the other sub, Sisso, hits the woodwork in injury
time! I'll take that point thank you very much, and I don't care if
we deserved to lose by five! We have dropped to 13th, but we
are still only five points off the play off places. Fulham have

sacked Paul Bracewell, and we have a week to prepare for Carlisle at the Mill.

26-1-00

It's going to be a skeleton back three on Saturday, Allardyce is banned. I am going to have to play Asko. If they stick it in the air, we will struggle. I am looking at reserve team options.

29-1-00

In the end, I decided to call up Danny Bacon from the reserves. He'll be on the bench today. I see Sammy McIlroy got the Luton job, maybe I should have applied! No, I couldn't leave Hazza right now; he's a good boss. It's back to the old routine today, off to the ground early, walking down Market Street. Kit out with Leathers, then a cuppa. He tells me about when Kenny Daliglish went on loan from Celtic to Cumbernauld United back in the very late 60's. Apparently Kenny, who went on to be one of the greatest British strikers of all time, was there for four months and didn't score a single goal or even have a single shot on target. Apparently Cumbernauld decided to play one of the best talents in the game in goal for his time there! Madness. Back to my selection dilemma, and I decide to go with Asko, despite the fact he worries me greatly.

Very random hour, I got a call just before I am about to submit the team. Asko's one match ban has started, so he cannot play. Thank god someone realised. Danny Bacon, you're in! Everything else seems in order, and I am giving Jorgy is his first start.

It feels like we have nicked that when a draw seemed the fairest result! Jorgy clinically gave us the lead, and then GK should have made it two. Onesy hit the bar from a tight angle just before half time. I was concerned with our back three flying into tackles all over the shop, so told them to calm it a bit – we cannot afford any more suspensions. As a result of that advice we were miles away from Tracey as he equalised for them. As ever though, if in doubt, get it to Onesimo. We did just that and he netted the winner with just ten left on the clock. Come on! The win lifts us up to 10th and Hazza even popped his head in to say he was "pleased with the result." We've got a week to prepare for Halifax away, and it is about time we beat them.

31-1-00

Fulham have appointed the Dutchman, Arie Haan. I wonder if the English game will start to go this way, lots of foreign managers taking the jobs where the is some money to spend. Chelsea have already started doing that over the last few years, Tigana has taken over at Wolves, Egil Olsen is at my old club, Wimbledon and Gerard Houllier is the man in charge at Liverpool. It will be interesting to see. At least it's not foreign chairman, which would be a nightmare! I see Bazza has won manager of the month; you cannot keep an old dog down. Talls is back in full training following his injury; I need him back in there.

2-2-00

I had my monthly lunch with Hazza today, scampi and fries as usual. He told me the board are still "delighted with my performance" which is good to know. I got to the training ground to hear that Hibs have put in a £10k bid for young Shaun Archibald. It's a rubbish offer, but the lad is a Hibs fan. I called Alex McLeish straight away and told him that I cannot stand in the kid's way, but I need more than £10k for him. How about £25k? Leathers let me know that Talls twisted his knee in training and is now out for three weeks. That is a blow.

4-2-00

Well, this is interesting. I got a call from Turner, telling me his source says Walter Zenga may be up for joining us as a player/coach. I'd have to let Wilko go, but Zenga is an absolute legend. I've agreed to have a chat with him about it. McLeish did the decent thing and came back with an offer of £25k, which I have accepted. A rare defeat for the reserves, whilst we are on the coach to Halifax. Danny Bacon was gutted; he is their skipper normally. He will be even more gutted when I tell him he is back on the bench tomorrow.

5-2-00

I got a phone call in the hotel from young Shaun, thanking me for letting him speak to Hibs. He has agreed terms. Good luck to the lad. I never got the call from Luton when I was playing, but if I had I would have been there in a shot and played for nothing. So, Halifax today. They are second bottom, but we haven't beaten them yet over three matches this season. Allardyce is back from suspension, so he will start. Other than that, I have decided to go with the same eleven as last week. Stace delivered a really good team talk, but I noticed Wilko was in a foul mood. He can't know, can he?

Thank god that is the last time we have to play them this season. Another awful match, no rhythm at all. Allardyce had a total 'mare on his return, he gave away a blatant pen – 1-0 down. Sisso hit a lovely equaliser, but we came in at half time 2-1 behind. I rattled some cages, brought on all three subs, but no response from the lads at all. Until the 90th minute that is, when Jonny Milner let fly and robbed us a point! We must improve!

8-2-00

Today was the day that I decided to let Wilko go. Zenga agreed terms, so it was something I had to front out. It was messy, he already knew all about it from somewhere and it proper kicked off. I let him say his piece, he deserved that much. That's football I guess – it could be me in that chair next week, hearing the same words from Hazza. Macclesfield appoint Colin Lee, Wolves to Macclesfield – that has go to hurt. I must resist the temptation to pick Zenga, no matter how good he looks in training. Bowler has not let us down at all this season, he has been superb. Next up, Plymouth. We owe them, we really owe them.

12-2-00

Ah, the Saturday morning buzz. The "Green Army" are in town. Kidder has been passed fit by Leathers; he will slot straight back into the back three instead of Dizzy. Other than Talls, we are at full strength today. They are currently sixth, so this could be a great win. Usual cuppa with Leathers, he told me he was pleased to see Wilko go, reckoned he was a bad influence. No card schools with Walter, right? I gave the lads a huge team talk, full of passion, one of my best. They were sent out about as fired up as they could be.

That's my boys! We dominated them! GK hit the post in the first minute, which is normally a sign that we are going to concede straight away. But no, Jorgy put us ahead with another clinical finish; he is looking like a shrewd signing. GK then hit the post again, and we continued to look superb for the first forty-five minutes. Onesy did seem a bit quiet though. The second half brought us three goals in six minutes, Jonny Milner hit a curler from the edge of the box, Allardyce tapped in after their 'keeper spilled a shot and then Clarkey made it four! They pulled two back late on, but the game was always ours. It's on again! We are up to tenth, only three points behind Northampton who are in seventh, and four points off York in fifth. Hazza was back to being "absolutely delighted." We have a big away trip to the leaders, Rotherham, next weekend.

15-2-00

We have been very focussed this week, if we can come away from Rotherham unbeaten then I will really start to believe we can be contenders. I do wish Talls was fit for this one.

18-2-00

The reserves beat Rotherham's reserves at the Mill. I hope that is a good omen. GK has picked up a knock in the last session before the match, fitness test tomorrow. If he is out, I might have to risk Talls.

19-2-00

It's a big day, today. GK fails his test with Leathers and Cisto is suspended, which means I have to change it up. I have to go with Asko at the back; it is about time he performed. In midfield, I have decided to drop Jorgy deeper into GK's position and bring in "The Blind" up top. The lads seemed really nervous at breakfast, I almost wished Wilko was around to help them relax; Zenga isn't really one for doing that.

Yes! Yes! Yes! I am proud to say I got it bang on today. Jorgy was absolute quality playing deeper and "The Blind" brought the best out in Onesy again. The Spaniard got us off to a great start with a header for 1-0. Then Jorgy, from Onesimo's corner, made it two. Somehow we let them back in it, Pratt scoring two quick goals to draw them level. I would have thought by now, teams would avoid fouling Onesy anywhere near the penalty area – Rotherham clearly hadn't realised and chopped him down again, so he got up, took aim and blasted yet another free kick home to put us 3-2 up! He really should have got his third just before the break, making a mess of a one on one with Pollit. The second half was tense; Bowler was having a shocker and looked like he could throw one in at any point. Luckily, "The Blind" restored our two-goal cushion and we continued to manage their main man, Leo Fortune-West. Eventually he did find some space though, and made it 4-3, but we managed to hold on for the win! I tell you what, we can get promoted, and I really believe that now. We are eighth and rising. Fish and chips for the missus tonight! Come on!

20-2-00

It's been a bad day on the South Coast. Alan Ball has been sacked at Pompey, Mel Machin has left Bournemouth. Good news for us though, our Thai lad has joined us today – I wonder if that will open up the Asian market to a new generation of Mansfield fans? I've told him he will be with the reserves initially, whilst he adapts to life in Nottinghamshire.

26-2-00

It has been a quiet week after the high of Rotherham. All eyes have been on Barnet, who come to us today. Sisso's out and Talls isn't back in full training yet and neither is GK. I might have to risk one of them, or I could turn to Cervera who hasn't figured much recently. Cisto is definitely back though, and he comes in for Asko. I got to the ground early, put the kit out with Leathers and we had a cuppa in silence, I think he has had a bad week outside of Field Mill. In the silence, I decided to risk GK, as Talls hasn't played for a month. I know it is a football cliché, but if we lose today it means the win against Rotherham was totally pointless. I told the lads as much in the team talk.

It wasn't much of a game, to be honest. We had eleven shots on target, and Onesy put us ahead in a very close first half. I was just saying to Stace how we needed that second goal when Jorgy headed home Cisto's corner. We didn't manage a clean sheet as they got a late lifeline, but it's another three points in the bag, more fish and chips for the missus and we are up to seventh!

I got home to the news that Steve Bould has been banned for 90 days for "assaulting" Steve Bennett after getting two yellows for Sunderland against my old side, Wimbledon. Wow, you don't see that very often and I always assumed it would be Martin Keown from that old Arsenal back four who would do something stupid. We have a week to prepare for Exeter away, can this run continue?

29-2-00

I am quite glad I don't work on the South Coast; Micky Adams has been fired from Brighton now! Sabitzer has picked up a knock in training; he is out for three weeks. On the plus side, Talls is back in full training, finally, and I think I will be bringing him back in for young Jonny Milner. I finally got some time in the evening to watch the Champions League for the first time this season. Arsenal beat Mallorca, away, which leaves them 3rd in their 2nd Phase group. Chelsea and United are playing tomorrow.↓

1-3-00

We had a nightmare training session today; both Allardyce and Cisternas got injured and will be out for a fortnight. Third Division Player of the Month also got announced, and yet again Onesimo has been overlooked. I don't think the appreciation for talent from abroad has quite filtered down from the Premier League yet. Harry Bassett has got the Bournemouth job, so I called my old gaffer to wish him luck. Chelsea beat PSV and United drew 0-0 with Parma. I find European games quite dull to be honest; I preferred the old knockout tournament.

2-3-00

Hazza took me out for our monthly lunch today, we had the usual. He is still "delighted" with me. He was "delighted" with me when we were 19th, and still "delighted" now we are 7th. Gary Megson has been fired from Stoke; I reckon they should give the job to Tony Pulis. Roy McFarland has taken over at Portsmouth.

3-3-00

Overnighter in Exeter tonight, thank god, as it is a four-hour coach ride. I have decided that Asko and Dizzy will have to come in to the back three and that Talls will give Milner a rest. We arrive at the hotel and hear that the reserves have beaten Exeter 3-1, Boulding getting a hat trick.

4-3-00

The team are well prepped and we had a decent breakfast together. Stace told me this story he had just read in *The Independent* about all the World of Leather stores are about to close. "Oh no, Leathers!" I shout across the tables, "Not only has your missus left you, now the family business is going under!" Credit to him, he actually laughed. On a serious note, where am I going to get my sofas from now? We have a good team meeting, where I explain to the lads that we need a really good March if we are going to stay in contention. They seemed pumped.

Well that wasn't the start to March I hoped for, what a slow, painful death that was. We were three down after twenty minutes, and then looked like we had just had the shit knocked out of us by Lennox Lewis. "The Blind" got one back just on half time, but nobody seemed to react. It all kicked off at the break, Stace proper laid into Bowler, who was having a shocker to be fair. Bowler was completely gone, I could tell, so I turned to Zenga, hoping he still had something in the locker. I also hooked Talls, who was way off the pace and suggested to Jorgy that he "wake the fuck up." Zenga certainly seemed to remember one part of his goalkeeping routine, picking the ball out of the net as he had to do that twice before he could even think about making a save. Milner got one late on, not that it mattered. Somehow their 'keeper got MOM and a ten rating, god knows who judged that, we barely had a shot on target. We were proper piss-poor tonight and it is going to be a very long coach ride home. That has dropped us to tenth again. A quick turnaround is needed, we have the Orient coming to the Mill on Tuesday, and they won today putting themselves back in the play offs.

7-3-00

I have to admit, Bowler has been giving me sleepless nights this week. He has had two shockers in the last three games, ever since I let Wilko go. Maybe there is a fairy-tale story for Zenga in all this, comes out of retirement to lead us to promotion? I have to change it up for the Orient, out will go Asko, Talls and Bowler and in will come Bacon, Milner and Zenga. No cuppa with Leathers today, he hasn't shown up – I am worried that behind the laughter in Exeter is a guy deeply depressed. I considered calling John Gregory for some advice on how to handle that, but saw sense. I tell the lads that they need to make it up to the fans today; a lot of Stags travelled down to Exeter with us and spent their hard earned cash on watching that shower of shit.

Well, that was the most bat-shit crazy game of football I have ever been involved in. I have no idea where to begin. How about the fact that we were 3-0 down, again, after 25 minutes? I had to hook Dizzy and Clarkey after 30 minutes and somehow we got it back to 3-3 before halftime, Milner, GK and even Cervera scoring his first goal for the club. Straight after the break, Onesy scored to make it 4-3 to us then GK hit the bar from distance. We all know what happens straight after we hit the bar, and sure enough they went down the other end to equalise and then go ahead to nick it back, 5-4. I don't know whether to cry because it hurts so much or cry at being part of one the best matches ever seen at Field Mill. Without stating the bleeding obvious, we need to stop conceding three plus goals a game as it is quite difficult to win if you need to score four every week.

11-3-00

I am still in shock from Tuesday to be honest, and the lads are completely drained – mentally and physically. It was a long coach ride to Darlington last night, and I am concerned for how we are going to react to those back-to-back defeats. Sisso is fit, so he will play. Clarkey just about keeps his place and Allardyce is getting thrown back into it even though he is only just back in training. Stace tried to rally them as best he could in the warm up but I think the last week has killed our spirit.

Yet another match where I wished I still smoked! We went behind early, and then Sisso and Clarkey repaid my faith and dragged us ahead, somehow. Then Ansah scored an identical second goal for them, and I totally lost it on the bench with our defending. Half-time arrived and I went for them in the changing room, deciding to cut the pressing, forget the offside trap and scrapped the zonal marking. It wasn't Onesy's day either, so I sent Jorgy on in his place. Somehow we managed not to concede another and Jorgy and "The Blind" scored one each to give us a 4-2 win. Goals galore as usual, value for money when you watch us play. That result lifted us back up to 9th and Hazza was "absolutely delighted Johnny, absolutely delighted." Ten games to go, ten cup finals if you like. Barry Fry next Saturday.

14-3-00

I read that Celtic have paid £6m for the England Striker, Emile Heskey. I remember when really good players went to Scotland. Amazingly, Charlton have sacked Alan Curbishley. I thought he was going to stay there for at least another ten years, I guess there is no such thing as a job for life anymore. Swansea's promotion hopes have been hit by the news that John Hollins has taken the Stoke job. I still think Pulis was the man to bring back the good times at the Potteries. Alan Ball is back, at Cambridge. Chelsea have splashed the cash again, £10m on a lad called Moniero who I have never heard of.

17-3-00

I drove down to London Road to watch the stiffs hammer Peterborough 5-0; the Thai lad got a brace. I wonder if he might have a part to play at some point?

18-3-00

So, Barry Fry, what do you have for us this time? I still have Jonny Milner and a 4-0 win over you! I bet that hurts him. I have slightly revised the tactics and I believe we are ready for battle. Cuppa with Leathers, he tells me a story about how Barry Fry and been totally bollocked by Karen Brady at Birmingham for an interview where he slated the board. Bazza was standing in just a towel whilst getting this bollocking; it must have been a great sight! He did a great job there though, to be fair to him. He might have bought 142 players and sold 146 – but he made over £1m profit doing it! Team talk was given by Stace today and the lads headed out pumped for the biggest ten games in my managerial career.

One down, nine to go! Zenga rolled back the years with a vintage man of the match performance. Clarkey gave us an early lead, one up after two minutes. Onesy doubled that, after great work from "The Blind." We defended well, not often I have been able to report that recently, and their goal came from a very dubious pen that the linesman gave. We got one of our own though, and Onesy, as ever, sent the 'keeper the wrong way for 3-1. Back in the play offs! Hazza was "delighted" and I've never seen Mr. Fry so quiet as we shared a pint after the match. Northampton away on Tuesday, the literal six-pointer.

19-3-00

Jimmy Quinn has been sacked by Swindon. I went down to Wembley today, with Hazza, to watch the League Cup Final, Liverpool and Chelsea battling it out. Two foreign managers are leading their sides out at Wembley for the first time in this competition. Chelsea came out on top, winning 2-1 after extra time. Quite an exciting match, it looks like it might be a season of near misses for the Mersey boys.

21-3-00

Northampton away, another huge test for us today. I'm a mixture of excitement and nerves. The coach journey down gave me a real insight into our lads. The younger boys are listening to music on their fancy portable CD players, young Milner seems to be right into that new band, Coldplay. Some of the older lads like Bowler and Kidder are reading the newspapers, though admittedly it is only Stace who has progressed past *The Sun and Mirror*. All the foreign lads, and I seem to have signed a few, are chatting away trying to improve their English together. It looks, from a distance, as we have some cliques in the group, but I am proud to say that isn't the case, these lads have high morale and a great togetherness. We got to the Sixfield and I told the lads the side before they got off the coach. They know what needs to be done. Same eleven as last time out, Bacon keeps his place.

Was that the perfect performance? Well, it wasn't far off! We got off to an absolute flyer when Onesimo headed home. He ran rings round them all game, created everything for us, setting up "The Blind" for 2-0. The lads were buzzing at half-time; I had to try and calm them down and told them just to get the ball to Onesy. I brought Jorgy on, he smashed one on to the bar before "The Blind" went on to get our third and fourth, his first hat trick in English football! They were totally shell-shocked, I don't think anyone expected us to come here and win 4-0. Hazza looks like he is about to burst and we are up to sixth in the table. It's going to be tough to keep everyone's feet on the ground as the lads start to sing; "We Are Going Up" on the coach home. Maybe boys.

Maybe. Macclesfield at home on Saturday, and I've decided to give the lads tomorrow and Thursday off.

22-3-00

I wake up and read about yet more sackings. Aldo has gone from Tranmere. My old mate, Lawrie Sanchez, has taken the job at Charlton and Swansea have gone for John Reames, who was manager at Sutton United. That seems like a strange decision, I would have thought they wanted someone with league experience, as they are right in the promotion hunt. By teatime it is reported that Gerry Francis has been shown the door at Loftus Road. After tea I got a call telling me that Norwich have offered a contract to Andy Roscoe, who will be out of contract at the end of the season. He can't even get on our bench at the moment, and a First Division club want him? I really don't want to start giving out contracts until the end of the season, which means I may lose a few if they get an offer elsewhere. I called Stace and spoke to him about this, he agreed that it could disrupt us and at least at the moment some of the lads will be playing to earn a new deal.

24-3-00

Transfer deadline day, today. Thank god I won't be tempted by anymore Swedish 17-year-olds or South American midfielders after today, and I can stop getting faxes trying to buy some of my players. I reckon they should only let transfers happen in the summer, and maybe at Christmas – imagine how much fun and drama that could create. The reserves beat Macclesfield 2-1. My only dilemma for tomorrow is whether to bring back Cisto for Bacon.

25-3-00

I barely slept; I must have played the match in my head about fifty times. I think we won twenty, lost fifteen and drew fifteen and all of them were laden with goals. I have decided that Cisto starts on the bench, as the back three were awesome on Tuesday. That means it is an unchanged eleven today. The town is buzzing as I walk down Market Street; they've not seen a season like this since the 70's apparently. Cuppa and kit with Leathers, he tells me this story about when he went to a Reading match a few years ago now and although the Royals won 4-1 he managed to miss all five goals. Leathers reckons that due to his late arrival he missed the first goal. Due to his craving for a burger and the long queue he missed two goals, one just before half-time and one after, the last goal he missed because he left early, but the real cracker Leather's story is that he actually managed to miss a penalty, as the bloke ran up to take it, he dropped one of his gloves and bent down to pick it up! Leathers cracks me up sometimes. I tell the boys what I saw in town today, and tell them, "to do it for them!"

Steamrollered! We started the game very nervously, but then "The Blind" put us ahead with a superb header, that boy is starting to remind me of a young John Fashanu. Clarkey doubled it for us with a carbon copy goal, and straight from kick off I hear a cheer and six of them are over in the corner celebrating again.

I must have got a dose of the Leathers as I missed it, talking to Stace about Clarkey's header! We are 3-0 up at halftime, and I asked Onesy what happened with the third one. "I get ball, I run, I run fast, I score again," he says. Simple! I told him he would be getting a rest in ten minutes. Jorgy was sent on for him, and Jorgy scored another clinical finish. They managed to get one back, finally beating Zenga who made some fine and fantastic saves today. The results came in whilst we were in the changing room and we are up to fifth now, just three points off second place with seven games to go. Stace told me that we are currently second in the form table. Hazza was "absolutely delighted" again. We are away to Southend on Saturday, and they are seventh.

26-3-00

I woke up early to the sound of the fax machine. A £300k bid for Jonny Milner arrived from Millwall. I thought the deadline had passed? I got straight on the blower to Keith Stevens at the Den and told him the shop was shut.

29-3-00

Swindon have gone for Paul Bracewell, as their new boss and Roscoe will join Norwich on a Bosman. Is he actually a good player and I haven't noticed? Carlisle played Plymouth tonight, 3rd against 9th. I could have done with a Plymouth win but Carlisle did them 5-1! I looked at our remaining fixtures, Lincoln are the only side right down the bottom. Shrewsbury and Chester have nothing to play for and Rochdale, Southend, York and Swansea are right in the promotion mix with us.

31-3-00

Overnighter to Southend, the coach was too quiet on the way down. I think nerves are really starting to kick in now. Either that or they were super focussed. Apparently Glenn Hoddle has walked out on Bury, leaving them bottom of Division Two and got the job at Tranmere. Incredible, and he probably thinks he is climbing the ladder. The reserves drew. Manager of the Month went to Dave Hodgson at Darlo, I've clearly been forgotten about, as has Onesimo who has been overlooked for Player of the

Month again. Big Nev Southall, and I mean big nowadays, got it down at Torquay, the only side in better form than us currently. Tommy Burns has taken a drive up the M4 from Reading to take the QPR job. I hope I sleep tonight.

1-4-00

We had a nice, light-hearted breakfast at the team hotel. Clarkey did a load of impressions to make everyone laugh. I liked his Chris Tarrant from *Who Wants to be a Millionaire*. His *Teletubbies* was pretty rubbish though. I told the lads it was the same eleven again and that we need to keep this run going!

So, we scored another four! Milner and "The Blind" got two each. The big problem was, they got six. That's right, six. Crazy. Their lad Neville Roach helped himself to four. I guess it was another one of those one-off freak games. It could have been twelve each I reckon. On the plus side, we are still sixth. We've let in 79 goals now, worse than Hull who are bottom. But we have scored 98, by far the most in the division. Certainly not dull, European football here. Rochdale next, they also need a win to keep their play off hopes alive. Hazza had a word on the way home, he won't have time for lunch tomorrow but he is still "delighted with my performance."

6-4-00

I was at the PFA Awards Dinner tonight at a swanky London venue, just like the old days. Robbie Fowler got the Player's Player Award, his Liverpool teammate; young Michael Owen got the runner up prize. That is one hell of a strike force that. Kieron Dyer got the Young Player of the Year award. They also chose the Third Division Team of the Year tonight, which felt a bit strange as there are 6 games left and it is the tightest division in Europe this season. Onesy was selected though, along with the Orient 'keeper, Damien Francis at Southend and Neil Tarrant at Rochdale. None of the others that they picked have really worried us this season, yet! Reading have bid £100k for Clarkey, so much for that transfer deadline quietening things down. "Leave my players alone, please," I politely tell their chairman,

Madjeski, at the dinner. "Try finding a manager here tonight, instead!"

7-4-00

Bollocks, Kidder is injured again. That weakens us instantly. Apparently one of the reserve team is also going elsewhere on a Bosman at the end of the season. Good luck to him. I didn't have time to read the papers today as all I was thinking about was Rochdale, three points and can we defend without Kidder?

8-4-00

I didn't sleep, again. The missus has got the right hump with me, keeping her awake with my tossing and turning. I presume Sir Alex, Arsene, Gerard all have sleepless nights as well. As well as Mansfield versus Rochdale it is FA Cup Semi Final day today. I remember playing against Luton in '88. I played really well that day, I still cannot believe I didn't even get in the squad for the final against Liverpool. It's great to see Fulham, Newcastle, Middlesbrough and my old club, Wimbledon competing for places at Wembley today, it makes a refreshing change. Cisto will come in for Kidder I have decided, Stace agrees with me. Cuppa with Leathers, I think we were both too nervous to have story time. Somehow I needed to find a way to get the lads relaxed and able to play their game. Great news broke before kick off; Kidder tracked me down and told me he wanted to play. I decided to trust him and dropped Danny Bacon to the bench so Cisto also started. We need a win here, obviously!

Christ, how the hell can we lose 6-1 at home and hope to get promoted? Changes all round next week. They absolutely killed us from start to finish. These tactics have got us in the promotion race, do I change them now? That result really hurts. I cannot even bare to look at Tarrant, whose hand I was shaking in London at the awards ceremony the other day. We are seventh with five to go, twelve goals shipped in two games. I am very tempted to go back to four at the back, but I will speak to the coaches and get their thoughts. Hazza had a word; "upset at the manner of the defeat," I think he said. Not a good time, Mr. Chairman, not a good time!

9-4-00

So it will be an all North East FA Cup Final as Newcastle trounced Fulham and Boro nicked it off Wimbledon at the death. Wigan have sacked John Benson. I'm still coming to terms with yesterday; it feels like a death in the family. My gut feeling is change the players, not the tactics. I need to freshen it up. I will no doubt spend the rest of the week thinking about it.

11-4-00

Jonny Milner has picked up an injury, so I will need to make changes anyway. Madjeski clearly ignored my polite request and is chasing one of our reserve team, Vaughan. I do recall signing him at the start of the season on a free; so I guess this will be profit!

13-4-00

I wake up to an early morning call from the Irish FA. They have called up Gary Tallon for their 'B' International against Turkey. I also get notified that Sabitzer has been called up to Austria's 'B' squad. It is great for them, but a right royal pain in the ass for me, as we need our eyes on the promotion prize. I decided on the side for Saturday early, and took the unusual step of telling the lads today. Bowler is back in goal; Allardyce, Gibbo and Clarkey have all been dropped. It is a gamble, but I needed to do something to get us back on track before the opportunity passed us by.

15-4-00

It's a nice short trip to Lincoln today, just over an hour. The reserves lost last night, and I have no idea if that is a good or bad sign. Clarkey, top lad, hid his disappointment at being dropped brilliantly and went around the coach geeing the lads up. Onesy seemed distracted; I hope he is not starting to think about next season. I have heard that a couple of Spanish clubs are interested in him. We arrived at Sincil Bank and some Stags were already there to cheer us off the coach. I gave the lads the biggest team talk yet, telling them that we are at a crossroads, one way leading to promotion, the other leading to heartache. Kidder piped up, "Err boss, that's not a crossroads, that's a T junction!" The lads pissed themselves and the tension seemed to be broken. Come on Mansfield!

"The Blind" got us going, opening the scoring after just four minutes. Onesy then hit the bar, great technique, before playing in Venetiaan for his second goal of the afternoon – he is on fire at the moment. It was great to come in at half time having not conceded for a change. I decided to change it to try and protect the lead, and go to a back four. But I changed my mind back again, telling myself, "Fuck this, we are winning!" I instruct Talls and Sisso not to bomb forward as much as a compromise. Half way through the second half they scored a pen and we were right on the ropes. We were struggling to contain them, so I went gung ho and pushed everyone forward again. Luckily for me, the Spaniard settled it in injury time. We only have four games to go, and this was the banker. It keeps us seventh, four points off third place, but also only four points separate eleventh spot and us! It is far too tight and I can see this going down to Swansea on the last game of the season. Hazza was back to being "absolutely delighted." Bury are the first side in England to have their fate decided, they have been relegated to Division Three. How on earth Hoddle got a new job after failing to turn that around, I will never know. York at home in seven days time, then Chester away on the sodding Bank Holiday Monday!

18-4-00

I decided to try and get Onesimo to commit to a new contract. If it gets announced he is leaving now the fans will lynch me and it will really unsettle the players. Annoyingly, he reassured me that he is happy at Mansfield, but he "does not wish to renegotiate a new contract at the current time." What the hell does that mean? Wigan have appointed Brian Kidd, who has abandoned ship at Barnet. Hartlepool has turned to Colin Addison.

19-4-00

I was able to catch some Champions League tonight. United booked their place in the semi's, beating Chelsea over two legs. They now join Barca, Marseille and Fiorentina in the hat.

22-4-00

The reserves seem to have stuttered recently, just a 1-1 draw last night. I had another sleepless night. I dreamt that Barry Conlon and Rodney Rowe took us to the cleaners and Bobby Mimms was bigger than the entire goal so there was no way past him. Arne played the fiddle on the coach trip to relax everyone. I have to say, I now hear Radiohead in a very different way. Kidder is banned, again, so Asko will come in in our only change.

Well, we needed some luck! First, Jorgy fluked the opener and it looked like the only way we were going to find a way past Bobby

Mimms in open play. It was the most one-sided half of the season (in our favour, that is) but he was stopping everything that came his way. We really needed that second goal. I threw on Jonny Milner for Talls and the young lad immediately won the corner that led to us getting a very dubious penalty. Onesy stepped up, Mimms went the wrong way and we had the two-goal advantage. They hit the woodwork, twice, late on and we got ourselves a huge three points! I went up to Mimms at the end of the game and told him he was "huge" in goal today. That win pushes us up to 5th with just three to play. The teams chasing us outside the play off spots are just two points behind though. Hazza is still "absolutely delighted." Chester away on Monday, I hope I don't regret the fact I only made one sub today.

24-4-00

I've barely had time to breath since Saturday. We were on the road to Chester bright and early today. They are 15th; we really must come away with all the points today. The lads seem pretty fresh considering the recent run of matches. No Talls though, he has had to join up with the Irish 'B' squad for that big piss up. Kidders is back though, he will slot back in for Asko, even though Asko put in his best performance for us last time out. Milner will replace Talls. Three games left lads, here we go!

It's been another one of those bad days. They ran away 4-1 winners. We were never in it, never. Luckily results have helped us, but with two games to go ourselves, Plymouth and Leyton Orient are all on seventy points and only two from those three can have a play off spot. But, above us, Torquay, Swansea and York occupy third, fourth and fifth on seventy-one points. This is tighter than a fat lady's blouse, as my Dad would say. Carlisle and Rotherham were promoted today, well done to them. Hull and Roy Evans were relegated to the Conference.

25-4-00

Cisto picked up a knock last night that will keep him out of the Shrewsbury game on Saturday. Steve Bruce has been sacked as manager of Huddersfield. This is starting to feel like the biggest week in the history of the club. I am starting to think we are either going to win automatic promotion or miss the play offs completely. Talls picked up his 'B' cap tonight, losing 2-0 to Turkey.

29-4-00

Decisions, decisions. I think I might have to bring in Asko for Cisto and Talls in for Jonny Milner. I also need a big performance from our main man, Onesimo. If we win today, it will not settle anything, but if we lose it might be over. God, I hope the boys get out there and give the fans something to remember! Cuppa with Leathers, he does everything to try and take our minds off it. He reckons we will be heroes by 5pm today, I hope he is right.

Well, I asked for a classic Mansfield performance and I guess a 5-3 win certainly counts as one of them this season. Two each after twenty minutes, I got the lads pressing in midfield again in the second half. GK and "The Blind" responded brilliantly, putting us 4-2 ahead. I decided to give Onesy a kick up the backside for next week, by subbing him early. Milner, on as a sub again, scored the fifth straight after coming on. Of course, they scored a third but it's another three points secured and we are up to fourth! Swansea now sit just outside the play offs, meaning they must beat us next week to keep their season alive. Torquay should beat Brighton to take the final automatic spot, but if they do not then there are five of us still with a chance of jumping in there. Hazza had been, I guess, on the brandy and was "absolutely delighted." Swansea, we are coming for you.

2-5-00

Wilkinson at Carlisle got Manager of the Month, fully deserved. The way they have chased down Rotherham has been superb. Lunch with Hazza at a slightly more posh place in town, we both have pasta. He is still "delighted with my performance."

3-5-00

Onesimo has started every game since he joined us, scored over thirty goals and now he gets injured! Leathers may as well have kicked me in the bollocks instead of telling me that he is out for three weeks, it would have hurt less. The lads were in shock when they heard, it is a massive blow. I started to think about the Thai lad that has been doing well in the reserves, maybe now is the time? Leathers popped back in later to tell me that Talls also has a knock, fuck! The day got even worse when Hartlepool try to unsettle us by putting in a bid for young Danny Bacon. This is not what I wanted in the build up to the Swansea game. I tried to relax in the evening, watching Barca beat United 2-1 at the Nou Camp on TV. Yeah, the Thai lad. I will tell him in the morning.

5-5-00

Overnighter to Swansea, and to be fair to Hazza he put us up in the Grand Hotel, which was much better than we are used to. We had dinner as a squad and I gave a little speech, thanking everyone there for their efforts so far and asking them for one more push tomorrow. I've decided to start the Thai lad. SB we call him, as I still cannot say his name right. I know it is a huge gamble, but Swansea is the Las Vegas of Wales. Milner will come in for Talls.

6-5-00

I slept like a baby, I think I knew deep down that there is nothing more I can do and that it is now out of my hands. Today will either end in glory and automatic promotion, misery and we miss out on the play offs or limbo, where we have at least two more matches to play. I gave each of the staff a little good luck memento and delivered my final team talk of the regular season.

Let me take you through the game. We started brightly, bang on it and then Venetiaan absolutely owned one from 25 yards and we're ahead. Our work rate was unbelievable; we were winning every single individual battle out there. Half time came, and I refused to hear any of the scores from the other grounds, I felt it was better just to focus on our next forty-five minutes. I told the lads that the next half of football will go a long way to shaping their place in the history of this famous old club. An hour was gone and Swansea were pushing us back deeper and deeper. I looked at the bench, starting to wonder what I could change to ease the pressure. There was no need! "The Blind" scored two in two minutes to get another hat trick and put us out of sight! They threw everything they could at us in the last fifteen, and for once we didn't even look like conceding. The whistle went and the lads all piled on top of Venetiaan, who was our hero in the absence of Onesimo, we had made it to at least the play offs! I asked Stace to go and find out the score in the Brighton Torquay game. He came back with the news I expected, Torquay won 2-0 and will finish third, in the final automatic spot. I tell the lads in the changing room how proud I am, but we have more to do. It's us, York, Plymouth and Southend. We will be away at Roots Hall next weekend. They've done the double over us so far this season, so it is time to change that. Hazza stuck is head round the door, "absolutely delighted lads, absolutely delighted!" Rotherham held on to win the title, it's nice knowing we beat the champions, convincingly, at their place. Now, what chance Onesy and Talls being fit at some point over the next two games?

10-5-00

United wrapped up the Premier League title on Sunday. Another back-to-back title for Sir Alex, and he as a Champions League Final to look forward to as well as United came from behind to knock out Barca in the semi. No team has ever defended the Champions League. I am more concerned about how we are going to turn the tables on Southend. Cisto is looking fit again, but I am reluctant to change the back three that did so well down in Wales. Talls is back in light training.

12-5-00

Overnighter in Southend again, I am obsessed with stopping Roach. That 6-4 defeat here is still haunting me. Talls isn't going to be fit enough to start, I'll have to leave him out and Onesy is nowhere near ready.

13-5-00

This is it, then. I decide that I will happily take a scoring draw back to the Mill. The lads are ready, they are well drilled. I tell them to go out and enjoy it, which is the reward for a great season. Same eleven as at Swansea, hopefully the same result.

Okay, we have a mountain to climb now, I admit that. But, it is not impossible. They beat us 3-1, but Clarkey hit the post at 2-1 down so it could have been completely different. Fucking Neville Roach! He scored again. Their 'keeper was superb; it just wasn't our day today. Sisso scored a great pen to give us an away goal, but how their lad stayed on the pitch after that I do not know. Shocking decision. It all comes down to Wednesday now. Plymouth edged the other game, 3-2.

17-5-00

Credit to the boys, they have worked hard this week. Their heads have been up; they will give it a proper go. I took yesterday off and left them with Stace. I took some time to reflect on the weekend and prepare myself for tonight. The plan is going to be simple, go hell for leather. We have an away goal, so 2-0 would be enough, but we know we don't often keep clean sheets so we have talked about needing to score four to go through. It's a big ask of the lads. Onesy has been declared 80% fit by Leathers, I tempted to start him. He will be on the bench at the very least; I will have a chat with Leathers and see what he thinks. Talls is back, he will definitely start. Onesy has been on my mind, why has his form dipped so much? Have Spanish clubs been tapping him up as his deal is coming to an end? Either way, the walk to the Mill was the last one of the season so I took my time and enjoyed it. Had my cuppa with Leathers, he was surprisingly gung ho. He said there was no point in saving Onesimo for a final that isn't coming, so I may as well give him a chance to say goodbye to the fans as he is probably going in the summer anyway! Gung ho or totally defeatist, not sure. Onesy is starting anyway! There is a different atmosphere in the changing room tonight. We are the total underdogs, there is no pressure on us and the lads are using that to their advantage. This might be the last time some of these boys grace the field at Field Mill. I refuse to get too caught up in those thoughts, and set about instilling some confidence in them. "Score early and they will panic!" I say, "and if they score it changes nothing, we still have to attack and we have as much chance of scoring four as we do two." And with that, they headed down the tunnel.

Football can be a game of such fine margins. A few inches here, a bit of luck there, a different decision by a referee. We came out of the blocks fast tonight, we really went at them in the way I hoped we would. Onesy went really close after fifteen, forcing Prudhoe to tip it wide. Then it happened, we went behind. Whyte found space, and scored after twenty-five minutes. The crowd went quiet, but then let out an almighty roar that brought hairs up on the back of my neck. Onesy must have decided at that point to give the fans something to remember the season by and went for the kill. Forty minutes were on the clock when he picked the ball up in the centre circle, ran half the length of the pitch amazingly unchallenged before driving the ball home. 1-1 at half time. "We could do this lads, we could do this!" I shout in the changing room. I turned to Milner and Clarkey in the second half, two Mansfield boys, could they save us? We went hammer and tongs at Southend, Onesy was trying everything. Seven minutes were left when Onesimo volleyed the ball goal wards from 30 yards. It clipped the bar and went over. So close! Moments later, he picked it up in midfield, sprinted past Roget, blasted it towards the top corner and scored the last, excellent goal of a hell of a season for Mansfield Town FC. We lost 2-1 on the night, but boy did we give them a fright. It was over, and the ref brought us to our collective knees by blowing the final whistle. We were superb tonight, but it wasn't our time.

I got all the lads and all the staff to do one final lap of the ground, thanking the Stags for their amazing support and patience throughout the season. By the time we finished, Hazza was by the tunnel, putting a brave face on it. "Sorry Hazza" I said, "it wasn't to be." "Johnny lad," he replied, "look around, they love us again. I am absolutely delighted! Thank you!" We trudged back into the changing room and I stuck my head round the away door where celebrations were in full swing. I offered my congratulations to Alan Little, and their skipper Simon Coleman.

I went back into ours and looked around. The lads were shattered, it was silent. I went around each one and shook their hands, and thanked them for giving me everything. Some of them could barely look at me, and those that could got a special word. "Bowler, the way you came back from being dropped was a credit to you lad." "Danny, son, you're 19. You'll get more nights like this and others will go your way!" "Sisso, you have grown up this year to be a leader of men, it brings a tear to my eye." "Clarkey, you are the perfect professional, thank you." Then finally, the One who gave us all so much hope and belief, Onesimo Sanchez. "Onesy, my lad, you are the best striker I have ever had the pleasure of working with. Even better than Terry fucking Gibson!" I thanked all my staff and walked out of the Mill, gutted that the season is over but very proud of our achievements. Time for a holiday, I think!

25-5-00

So I am writing the final entry of this season's diary from the sun lounger in Marbella. Just over a week has passed and it's a good time to reflect on my first season as a manager. I watched the Champions League Final in the bar last night, United fell at the final hurdle. Fiorentina beat them 3-2. Still nobody has been able to defend the title. I didn't watch the FA Cup Final on Sunday; it was too soon for me to be able to bare watching a game. Boro beat Newcastle 1-0 after extra time.

So how can I sum this up? Highlights? Beating the Posh 4-0 at their place was amazing. Going three at the back for the first time after we went down to ten men at Shrewsbury was a game changer. Beating the eventual Champions, Rotherham, at their place was a great buzz. Scoring 113 goals! The negatives? Those back to back defeats at Southend and at home to Rochdale where we shipped twelve goals cost us. One point out of that and we would have been promoted. Losing to Wrexham in the Autoglass, we would have gone on to win it the way our form picked up. Other than that, no regrets. We've played my way, we have way overachieved what was asked of us at the start of the season and we have entertained our paying public. For me, the star was obviously Onesimo – 40 league goals in 42 games. Incredible. But if we had signed Kidder sooner, who knows. The fans have voted him in 3rd place as player of the year, behind Bowler and obviously their first choice, Onesy.

As for me, on to next season if Hazza still wants me. I'll try and keep the bulk of the lads together and give it another bloody good go next season. Now, back to my beer!

JOHNNY COOPER, CHAMPIONSHIP MANAGER
The Second Season Syndrome
(according to Championship Manager)

Chris Darwen

The sequel, "Johnny Cooper, Championship Manager: The Second Season Syndrome" is now available on Amazon.

10221641R00079

Printed in Great Britain
by Amazon.co.uk, Ltd.,
Marston Gate.